DON'T KILL THE MESSENGER

How America's Valiant Whistleblowers Risk Everything in Order to Speak Out Against Waste, Fraud and Abuse in Business and Government

DONALD RAY SOEKEN

ISBN: 1492898090
ISBN 13: 9781492898092
Library of Congress Control Number: 2013919326
CreateSpace Independent Publishing Platform
North Charleston, South Carolina

TABLE OF CONTENTS

PREFACE

Thirty-five years in the making, this book got its start on an autumn afternoon in 1978, when the author first realized that "blowing the whistle" often carries severe penalties for those who dare to speak out against waste, fraud and abuse in government and business.

Although I never dreamed on that long-ago afternoon that I'd one day write a book about whistleblowers, there's no doubt that my understanding of the federal workplace changed greatly during an hour-long interview I conducted that day with a deeply troubled U.S. Department of Transportation (DOT) employee.

It was then that I learned – in stark, heartrending detail – how the Executive Branch of the U.S. Government was using forced "fitness-for-duty" psychiatric examinations to discredit (and in many cases, to financially destroy) federal employees who attempted to "go public" with reports of workplace abuse of one kind or another.

During the period (late 1970s) in which I interviewed the former DOT employee (she'd been forced to accept "disability retirement" and then to live on a meager $300-a-month benefit), these fitness-for-duty psychiatric exams were all too often being used as a way to prevent federal workers from speaking out about wrongdoing in their agencies.

As I learned more about this Orwellian assault on citizens who were usually involved in nothing more nefarious than being honest about abuses which sometimes cost the taxpayers millions, I began to ask myself how such repressive tactics differed from the outrageous human-rights violations then occurring frequently in the Soviet Union.

Were the agency supervisors who forced their workers to take psychiatric exams really any different from the commissars who regularly sent truth-tellers off to break rocks in the notorious Soviet "gulags"?

As a U.S. Public Health Service social worker who'd been raised on a Kansas farm and taught to uphold the staunch moral principles of mainstream American Lutheranism, I was both alarmed and outraged by the injustice of a system that could destroy the livelihood of a loyal federal employee who'd spoken out against fraud in the workplace.

During the years that followed my introduction to such "whistleblower reprisal," as I dug more deeply into the abuse of power that occurred with these forced exams, I gradually became convinced that the whistleblowers being injured by them deserved better treatment.

And I *said* as much – during lengthy congressional hearings on Capitol Hill and during interviews with such publications as the New York *Times* and *Parade* magazine.

Although the practice of requiring forced psychiatric exams was eventually prohibited in the executive branch of government by new laws, my interest in helping to defend whistleblowers against reprisals grew stronger with each passing year.

Writing for hundreds of U.S. newspapers (including the Washington *Post*) in his syndicated column in 1985, famed investigative reporter Jack Anderson described my early efforts to help whistleblowers tell their stories by listing several of my high-profile cases in which the struggle to help protect truth-tellers was both stark and dramatic.

"Soeken has treated hundreds of whistleblowers," wrote Anderson, before detailing the case histories of "an editor of a Health and Human Services Department publication who reported wrongdoing to a congressional committee and, thereafter, was fired on trumped-up charges that he was a brain-damaged alcoholic" . . . and a "woman [federal employee] who was labeled 'unfit' by her superiors after she revealed their rampant sexual harassment."

In the more than 25 years since those early struggles, I've done my best to help literally thousands of whistleblowers in their efforts to speak out against fraud, waste and abuse in both government and business.

Along the way, I've been part of some of the country's most harrowing, headline-making news stories – white-knuckle narratives in which heroic whistleblowers risked everything in order to stun the nation with their reports of wrongdoing in high places.

Many of those dramatic stories will be found in this book. Among the most gripping tales in the pages you're about to read are the highly suspenseful account of a supremely honest Federal Bureau of Investigation agent (Fred Whitehurst), who went public with reports that the agency's major national crime lab had been "doctoring" lab tests in order to help prosecutors win convictions . . . along with the daring story of a defense contractor-employee (Brian Hyatt) who refused to keep quiet about wholesale fiscal fraud that threatened to put America's nuclear-missile capability at risk.

Other stories in this book include the saga of a valiant U.S. Marine Corps officer (Franz Gayl) who made national headlines by blowing the whistle on the Corps' failure to supply its own troops with state-of-the-art armored vehicles that could have saved hundreds of lives during the Iraq War . . . and the equally compelling factual account of U.S. Department of Agriculture analyst Linda Lewis, who refused to allow her supervisors to whitewash managerial breakdowns that threatened the integrity of procedures designed to test the ability of the nation to protect its food supply during a nuclear-energy accident.

In each of the chapters that follow, I've done my best to accurately portray the high stakes that were at work . . . while also documenting the ways in which I tried to help the struggling whistleblowers who were involved. In many cases, that help involved nothing more elaborate or complicated than simple counseling and friendship – while in others, I found myself helping the affected whistleblowers to find affordable legal assistance, being an expert witness, or news media coverage, or even adequate food and shelter.

As *Parade* magazine noted in a Jack Anderson article about my continuing efforts to help whistleblowers survive the reprisals they so often face, one especially effective resource during the past 25 years has been "The Whistlestop" – a farmhouse in the hills of West Virginia where many of the truth-tellers I've counseled lived rent-free for months at a time while putting their lives back together.

Describing the "safe house" we were able to create in a peaceful Appalachian setting, *Parade* noted that "at his home away from home – a farm in the lush hills of West Virginia – [Soeken] has created a haven for whistleblowers. He calls it, 'The Whistlestop'. Its mission is to give those who tell the truth a place to come for respite when they are persecuted for their honesty. Why would a whistleblower need the equivalent of a safe house? Because, while the federal government may have stopped trying to prove whistleblowers are crazy for speaking up, it still does its best to drive them crazy after the fact."

During a career of nearly 30 years as a psychiatric social worker at the United States Public Health Service (from which I finally retired in 1994 with the USPHS equivalent rank of a captain in the U.S. Navy), I often struggled hard to balance my responsibilities as a government employee with my volunteer efforts as an advocate for and a counselor to whistleblowers. Today I feel very fortunate that I was able to continue both activities without losing my effectiveness in either realm. It wasn't easy, however – and there were many times, as I watched distressed truth-tellers suffer from painful reprisals, that my faith in the checks and balances of the U.S. government and the ethics of corporate management were severely tested.

This book is the story of that struggle to help protect vulnerable whistleblowers from self-destructive behaviors and crippling despair, while also helping them find the resources they needed for physical and emotional survival. More than three years in the writing and editing, *Don't Kill the Messenger!* could not have been completed without the devoted efforts of many other people . . . including, especially, the valiant whistleblowers who spent countless hours describing and reflecting on their struggles as people who dared to stand up and speak out against wrongdoing. But I also owe a debt of gratitude to my editor, Tom Nugent, who pushed me continually to dig for more detail, fill in more background and find more revealing information from hundreds of historical records and living sources sometimes located as far away as New Zealand. I'm also grateful to my longsuffering wife Karen, who never stopped encouraging me – and to my now-grown offspring, son Jeff and daughter Beth, who never stopped supporting me, in spite of my long hours away from home.

(I should also point out that in two chapters of this book (Chapter 1 and Chapter 8), it was necessary to protect several former federal employees from potential injury by changing their names. Although those few names were altered in order "to protect the innocent," I want to emphasize the fact that *all of the factual material (descriptions of incidents, quotes, etc.) contained in those two chapters and in all the other chapters is 100-percent accurate.*)

I also want to offer a special thanks to all the energetic and cheerful volunteers who have helped in creating and sustaining the non-profit Whistleblower Support Fund (WSF) (http://whistleblowing. us/about-us/our-history/). Launched more than a decade ago by this author, the Fund sponsors the Whistleblower Support Center and the International Whistleblower Archive and also strives to directly support and offer expert witness testimony to whistleblowers in both corporate and government organizations. The mission of the WSF is to help protect free speech – while also protecting all Americans from on-the-job abuse, harassment and reprisals for telling the truth about workplace abuses.

In the spirit of Martin Luther, along with Jack Anderson and all those brave Americans who have risked so much in order to protect our freedoms over the years, I sincerely hope that you will find this book useful in understanding why we must protect our truth-tellers for our *own* sake – and for the sake of generations that are yet to come!

—Donald R. Soeken, LCSW-C, Ph.D.

Ellicott City, Maryland

ONE

BEGINNINGS

I remember the moment when Wilma cried.

It was a mild, early-autumn afternoon in October of 1978, and I was hard at work in my office at the U.S. Public Health Service Outpatient Clinic, located only a few blocks from Capitol Hill in Washington, D.C.

In those long-ago days, I was a very dedicated and very serious-minded mental health counselor for the federal government. Only 36 years old, and with the ink still drying on my Ph.D. and my license as a Licensed Certified Social Worker, I'd been assigned to a job I loved: helping federal employees deal with the life-shattering effects of mental stress and mental illness. As a German-Russian-American farm kid who'd been raised in small-town Kansas, my ideals had been shaped by my upbringing as a Lutheran . . . but also by my early years in a farm family that put great emphasis on such time-tested values as honesty, responsibility and hard work. With those two powerful life lessons in my background – the legacy of Martin Luther and also the legacy of the prairie farmer – I was passionately committed to my vocation as a healer.

For the past six months or so, I'd been bringing these concerns home with me and worried about what to do to help federal employees deal successfully with mental-health issues that often left them feeling hopelessly depressed and paralyzed. The work was far from easy.

Indeed, counseling federal workers with mental problems often meant confronting their often agonizing pain with them, while also doing my best to help with urgent problems such as stresses at the workplace and at home so that they could continue to have some relief. The cases I handled were often nerve-wracking and dauntingly complex . . . and I knew that this one would be no different.

On this particular afternoon, I'd agreed to counsel a deeply troubled former employee at the U.S. Department of Transportation (DOT) . . . an employee who had fallen into a deep, crippling depression in recent months. Wilma Jefferson was clearly in trouble, and her chaotic life was slowly coming apart at the seams. She had acknowledged this fact to me during several earlier counseling sessions – and yet she kept stubbornly insisting that she wasn't "mentally ill" at all, and that she had been "perfectly competent" to perform her job as a secretary at the DOT.

But her bosses hadn't agreed with her: six months before her visit to me in October of '78, they had concluded that she was mentally ill and had insisted that she be placed on "disability retirement" . . . where she would be required to live on a meager disability payment of only $300 a month.

"Dr. Soeken," she stammered now, between wracking sobs, "I need you to understand that all of this happened because my supervisor made me take that 'fitness for duty' psychiatric exam. *That's* why I lost my job. They rigged the results of that exam, and I am *not* crazy. And do you know why I was ordered to take the test in the first place? It's because I blew the whistle on all the 'overtime padding' that was going on in my department!"

Listening carefully, I handed Wilma a Kleenex, then waited patiently while she blew her nose. At the same time, I realized with growing alarm that her complaints about being "railroaded" out of her job might actually have merit. Had losing her livelihood, merely for telling the truth, punished her? As a patriotic American who loved his country deeply, I didn't want to entertain the idea – not for a single moment – that the people who managed a major federal agency like the DOT might be willing to destroy an employee's career in order to prevent her from going public with a disclosure that could embarrass them.

Some background: During several previous interviews at my office near the Capitol, Wilma Jefferson – a 38-year-old, African-American secretary with an outstanding performance record up to then – had continued to insist that her bosses at DOT had used their "psychiatric fitness for duty exam" as a way to drive her out of her GS-5 federal job. At first I had assumed that her complaint was a mere rationalization, a way of denying that she was mentally ill.

I requested permission to review all of her employment files from the Office of Personnel Management. After asking for the files and waiting several months, we decided to seek congressional help. Wilma had been to the office of Senator Jacob Javits and found that his staff was very helpful, even though she did not live in New York State. I contacted the staff person and asked her to request the files, and she managed to obtain them in less than a week.

But after studying her employment file in great detail, I could not conclude that Wilma suffered from "paranoid schizophrenia" – or that her performance in the months leading up to her "retirement" had been anything less than stellar. Her employee evaluations had been consistently high, and her attendance and punctuality scores had been nearly perfect. So what was actually going on here?

Deeply puzzled, I waited while she regained her composure. Then I leaned forward in my government-issue swivel-chair and concentrated on every word I was hearing from Wilma.

"They were *stealing*, Dr. Soeken. One of the supervisor's secretaries was routinely padding her hours, and I went public with it. I reported everything to DOT Security. And do you know how my bosses responded? Instead of thanking me for reporting the overtime padding – which amounted to nothing less than stealing from the American taxpayers, if you think about it – they forced me to take a physical exam, and when I passed that, they forced me to take a psychiatric exam. And I was so nervous and upset that day . . . well, I was just scared to death, and I'm sure I probably flubbed a couple of questions as a result."

While reviewing her file, I found that after she had been sent to a "contract psychiatrist" who did *not* find the psychiatric illness that would have allowed the agency to "retire" her, the DOT arranged for a review of his exam by its own agency psychiatrist. This second psychiatrist added his *own* diagnosis – without ever seeing the patient – of "paranoid schizophrenia." DOT then forwarded that diagnosis to the Office of Personnel Management, which proceeded to retire her for life on $300 a month in disability income.

Wilma paused as she described what had been done to her, and her mild brown eyes suddenly flashed with outrage. "They manipulated my case," she groaned, "in order to come up with their 'paranoid schizophrenia' diagnosis, and I did not even see the psychiatrist. And as you can see clearly from the original medical file, that exam actually showed I could *not* be retired on a psychiatric disability. But so what? Those government psychiatrists can do anything they want, and once they make that diagnosis of mental illness, the next step is disability retirement. There's no appeal, and there's nothing you can do to get your job back."

Nodding, I thought for a moment. "So, you're telling me that they forced you out the door, correct? They took your career and most of your income, merely because you blew the whistle on the overtime fraud in your department?"

She was dabbing at her eyes with the Kleenex. "That's exactly right, Dr. Soeken. They ruined me! I've got no job now, and the disability money isn't nearly enough to keep me and my family going. They destroyed me for no other reason than speaking out against the theft.

"I blew the whistle, and now I'm paying for it." She gazed at me in anguish, and it was easy to see the pain burning in her eyes. "Dr. Soeken, they used the mental health system to wipe out a whistleblower. It's as simple as that . . . and I thought that kind of thing only went on in the Soviet Union!"

Burying her face in the Kleenex, she wept unashamedly. She was a broken woman – no wonder she'd sunk into "clinical depression" during the past few months. Watching her sob, I struggled with a growing sense of anxiety. I believed her story, and what if Wilma Jefferson had been run out of her job because she'd insisted on telling the truth? What would *that* say about the ethics and the morality at work in the U.S. Department of Transportation?

Suddenly, I realized that I was sailing into uncharted waters.

If the courageous woman in the chair across from me was reporting these events accurately, I knew I wouldn't be able to participate any further in the government's deceitful vendetta against her. Somehow, I would have to find a way to challenge the findings from the psychiatric fitness for duty exam and then help her to win reinstatement as a GS-5 federal employee.

I also realized – in a bone-chilling moment of very frightening insight – that Wilma's case was hardly unique. If the federal bureaucrats at DOT had used the fitness for duty exam as a way to get rid of her, they would surely be willing to employ the same tactics against other employees they disliked . . . *as well as employees who tried to blow the whistle on waste, fraud and abuse within the government.*

"Wilma," I told her as our session ended, "I want you to know that I'm going to do everything I can to help you. It won't be easy . . . but I'm going to find you a good *pro bono* lawyer, and I'm going to talk to a couple of friends of mine in the news media. If you were actually driven out of your career because you told the truth, we will find a way to let the public know it – and we won't quit until you've been vindicated and gotten your job back!"

Although I didn't know it at the time, I'd just taken the first step on the long road to becoming an American whistleblower.

I'd also begun what would eventually turn into a 40-year career as a mental health counselor who specializes in helping whistleblowers to survive the experience of speaking out against waste, fraud and abuse in government and business.

Looking back from the distance of three decades, I often find myself wondering how I wound up as the "Whistleblower Shrink" – a mental health professional who spends most of his working hours trying to assist those brave Americans who choose to "go public" with their reports of wrongdoing in the workplace.

In a way, I guess you could say that my "whistle-blowing career" actually began during some nerve-rattling conversations I'd had with my old Grandpa Henry, way out there in small-town Lyons on the Kansas prairie.

I've never forgotten those deeply frightening occasions on which Henry would come stomping up onto the front porch of our family's farmhouse, growling and muttering and determined to ask me a deeply disturbing question: "Okay, Donnie. *Jawohl!* How many cows you got out in the field today?"

"What, Grandpa?" Puzzled and nervous, I would stare distractedly past his broad shoulder to the ocean of wheat that surrounded our white-clapboard farmhouse – a rippling sea of wheat that stretched to the distant horizon, pale gold and bending gently beneath the prairie wind.

"Cows, Donnie! I'm askin' you how many cows you got out there in the field!"

I gaped at him, this roughhewn German in the bib overalls and the mud-spattered fedora: Henry Soeken, the second son of the ancient Soko Soeken. Soko had once been the most stubborn man in all of Bagband near Aurich, Lower Saxony, Germany, according to local legend. He'd also been a lieutenant in the Prussian Army, and a bold-hearted critic of the German Kaiser. Indeed, the valiant Soko had gone so far as to tell his commanding officer that he would always fight to protect the Fatherland – but that he would *not* be part of an invasion of nearby Austria, since he regarded this step as an unethical act of military aggression. And he was as good as his word. When the invasion took place, Soko became one of the members of the Soeken clan to immigrate to America, back in the late Nineteenth Century.

Henry Soeken was a hard-nosed, no-nonsense wheat farmer, and his tough-minded ways were easy to understand . . . given the fact that his father Soko had ridden "below decks" on an economy-class ticket aboard a jam-packed freighter full of immigrants across the storm-tossed Atlantic to America. Soon after completing that harrowing voyage – and accompanied by his new wife and his brand-new infant son – the indomitable Soko had endured a three-day odyssey aboard a soot-belching Missouri Pacific train to their new wood-plank cabin near Claflin, Kansas.

After reaching his rough-built prairie home in the summer of 1883, Soko had gone to work with brutal intensity . . . and had assembled the first Soeken homestead by hand, during endless years of backbreaking labor. Was it really any wonder that his humorless and fiercely driven son Henry would demand the same kind of iron dedication in *his* sons and grandsons, as they struggled to manage their own farmsteads and survive in the area around Lyons, Kansas (Population: 3,732) where I grew up?

How well I remember the fear I felt, as the somber-eyed old man in the bib overalls stepped onto the worn planks of the porch and scowled at me. *I'm askin' you how many cows you got out there in the field!* Henry was an American citizen now, but his frown looked very German to me at that moment. A classic Kansas wheat-and-cattle farmer, my old grampa was all business – and armed with a pair of hands that felt like slabs of weathered oak. Henry Soeken had survived droughts and blizzards and plagues of swarming grasshoppers, during his six decades of wrestling with Mother Nature on the Kansas prairie. He was a tough-as-nails taskmaster, but I didn't really hold it against him; even as a youngster, I understood that he *had* to be that way, if he hoped to carry on the legacy of Soko Soeken as a successful wheat farmer in a world where you could lose your crops overnight, if you didn't "take care of business" from one moment to the next.

Make no mistake: Henry Soeken was a formidable presence. And now, out of the blue, he was asking me to tell him – at the tender age of ten – just how many cows my father was pasturing in the South 80!

I couldn't stall any longer. Slowly, I brought my gaze up to meet his, until I was looking directly into his wrathful eyes.

"I don't know, Grampa."

He was gaping at me.

"You don't know how many cows?"

"No, sir. I don't."

He reached over and gave the screen door a loud whack for emphasis: "*Jawohl!* If you don't know how many cows you got, how will you know if you *lose* one?"

Years later, long after I had become totally immersed in the struggle to protect the whistleblowers I counseled daily, his lesson would return to me and I would work furiously in order to make sure that not a single one of these brave truth-tellers got "lost" in the life-threatening process of reporting fraud, waste and abuse!

Make no mistake: I understood Henry, and I understood why he felt he had to be so tough and demanding on the people around him. And yet there was another side of my nature (my "non-Prussian," softer mother's German Russian side) that rebelled against his ironclad perfectionism and his merciless discipline. Years later, after I found myself "rebelling" against a federal bureaucracy that believed it had the right to destroy employees' lives in order to prevent them from speaking out about abuses, I would often wonder if that rebellion had begun as I went eyeball to eyeball with Grampa Henry on the porch of our Kansas farmhouse.

But all of that was still far in the future. What happened next was that I got lucky and won myself a football scholarship to Valparaiso University, way off in distant Indiana. For 18-year-old Donnie Soeken – the big offensive tackle with the size twelve shoes and the jumbo shoulder pads – it would be the start of a 30-year career as a Ph.D. social worker and counselor to some of America's bravest and most honest souls.

Although I never imagined it at the time, my theology degree at Valparaiso U. would also help to provide the inspiration for my decision to specialize in counseling truth-tellers who "crash and burn" because of the psychic stress that invariably accompanies the act of going public with reports of wrongdoing. Valparaiso is a Lutheran institution, after all, and I sometimes like to imagine that the great Protestant reformer had a hand in inspiring me to challenge some of the corporate and government powers that run this country. Once in a great while, when I'm giving a speech or an interview somewhere, I'll find myself grinning like the schoolboy I once was, as I ask my curious listeners: "Say, did you know that Martin Luther was actually one of our very first whistle-blowers? He nailed his report on waste, fraud and abuse in the Church to the Cathedral door!"

Looking back on those long-gone college days, I'm sure my Lutheran background played at least a small part in my later willingness to "challenge authority" . . . even if most of my values had actually been shaped by my youthful experience as the son of a long line of incredibly

8

hard-working Kansas wheat farmers. Whatever the source of my will-ingness to "buck the system" and stand up for my patients rather than bowing to the dictates of the federal bureaucracy, however, it's also true that sheer luck also played a part in nudging me toward the national spotlight (and eventually onto the pages of the New York *Times* and *Parade* magazine) as a controversial social worker whose niche would so often involve counseling whistleblowers.

After earning a master's degree in social work at Wayne State University in Detroit and then later a Ph.D. in Human Development at the University of Maryland, I had signed on as a Licensed Certified Social Worker (LCSW) at the USPHS, way back in the late 1960s. Within a few years, I wound up as a field officer at the Mental Health Study Center of the National Institutes of Mental Health, which was located in Adelphi, Maryland, where I counseled patients and was fre-quently asked to assist workers who had developed mental issues while working for Uncle Sam.

So far, so good. By late 1977, I had been promoted to Chief Social Worker at the USPHS Outpatient Clinic in downtown Washington. And it was here, during the next year or so, that I became skilled at per-forming the kind of "mental health screenings" and "fitness for duty" exams which had eventually been used to force Wilma Jefferson (and many other federal workers like her) into early retirement.

By 1978, in fact, I found myself giving several of these "fitness for duty" exams each month. But when I questioned the unhappy workers who'd been required to take the exams, I discovered that most of them weren't mentally ill. In far too many cases, in fact, they had simply run afoul of their bosses – frequently after blowing the whistle on some il-legal or unethical practice that was taking place at the job site.

As you might imagine, I became deeply concerned that this psycho-logical tool was being used to drive whistleblowers out of the federal government.

Increasingly alarmed by this obviously illegal practice, I went and did some digging around in the history books in order to under-stand exactly how these forced exams had become standard operat-ing procedure within the federal government. After a few evenings spent wandering around the halls of Congress (only a short walk from my office), I learned that the U.S. Government had first launched the exams way back in the Truman Administration . . . after some of the McCarthy-era bureaucrats who ran the country concluded that they would be a powerfully effective way to keep federal workers in line.

(In that rather ugly era of American life, remember – with "witch hunts" and "loyalty oaths" the order of the day – there had been a great push on Capitol Hill to make sure that all federal employees were "clean" and free from the "spreading virus of communism." To achieve that goal, such clearly unconstitutional techniques as the "forced psychiatric exam" had become strictly routine.)

This was the backdrop, then, against which the Executive Branch of the government had promulgated rules which allowed the bureaucrats to eliminate "problem employees" by forcing them to take psychiatric fitness for duty exams and then declaring many of the test-takers to be "psychologically unfit" for continued federal employment.

Under the regulations which had first gone into place during the Truman Administration, the government had declared that a federal agency could require the Office of Personnel Management – the "OPM" – to psychiatrically evaluate and then retire those who were found to be "mentally ill," provided that the psychiatrist or mental health worker would pronounce the employee to be not fit for duty.

Those highly arbitrary – and in fact, illegal – regulations regarding Fitness for Duty Exams were still in place and operative in 1978, when I found myself performing many of the exams at the USPHS Outpatient Clinic in Washington. As I conducted the exams week after week, it had gradually become clear to me that most of the people who'd been sent to us for the exam were actually quite sane and sensible. In fact, as I discovered to my horror, most of the examinees were actually whistleblowers, or else they were simply employees who'd been unlucky enough to become embroiled in job disputes or personality conflicts with their bosses.

For a young man who'd been raised to honor the strictest standards of personal honesty, it was deeply disturbing to witness this clearcut abuse of the use of the U.S. Public Health Service, along with the psychological devastation it was causing among these frightened federal employees. Again and again I asked myself: What was my responsibility here? After much soul-searching, I decided it was my moral obligation to try and help these harassed employees as much as I possibly could. And within a few months, I was beginning to counsel many of them on ways to "fight back" against the government that was routinely trampling on their rights.

Soon I was sending these embattled truth-tellers to investigative reporter Indy Badhwar at the *Federal Times* and elsewhere (many of them would eventually end up telling their stories to famed investigative reporter Jack Anderson, at my suggestion). In many cases, the reporters involved would interview the employees and then write stories about the alleged employee-abuse that was occurring in various federal agencies.

I also began to evaluate my "exam" subjects with increased scrutiny during these "fitness for duty" probes, and we refused to certify any of them as "mentally ill" unless I and my psychiatrist supervisor uncovered indisputable evidence of such illness. Instead of producing the phony diagnoses that the various agencies obviously wanted from us, our USPHS mental health team increasingly began to return them to their jobs along with a certification statement that declared them fit for duty rather than unfit!

As the months passed and my refusal to participate in the "fitness for duty" diagnostic scam became more and apparent to the brass at the federal agencies, I grew increasingly anxious. Was I really doing the right thing in preventing these government supervisors from retiring employees they didn't want working for them anymore? And what about my *own* job security as a member of the U.S. Military? Because the USPHS is managed in a similar fashion as the Defense Department (we were even required to wear our military officers' uniforms to work one day per week), my future promotions – and even my retirement pension – might very well depend on job evaluations and performance ratings that could be influenced by some of the same agency managers I was refusing to "play ball with," as a citizen with different values than the Executive Branch.

Increasingly alarmed and uncertain about what the future might hold, I began asking the advice of seasoned human resources professionals and veteran human rights activists in the Washington area. Imagine my surprise when – at the urging of Wilma – I went to see Louis ("Louie") Clark, the director of the non-profit Government Accountability Project, a public-interest group that worked to reform abusive practices by various agencies in the federal government.

Full of reservations about my course of action, I told Louie all about the forced psychiatric exams and my disturbing discovery that many of the federal employees required to take them were actually whistleblowers who were being punished for speaking out against wrongdoing in their agencies.

I was amazed when he pointed out that I wasn't "imagining things" at all – and that the forced exams were in fact a violation of the Constitutional rights of every American citizen, regardless of where he or she worked! I knew Louie was a crackerjack lawyer (and also a Methodist minister) . . . and I was deeply shaken to hear him say: "Don, they're destroying lives every time they send one of these federal employees to you for a psychiatric fitness for duty exam.

"The Constitution absolutely prohibits them from forcing workers to submit to mental health exams – but the practice goes all the way back to Harry Truman, and they've been getting away with it for decades."

As I listened to Clark describe his outrage at these frequent violations of the U.S. Constitution, I began to wonder what country I was living in. All at once, a brutal fact had come shockingly clear: My federal government was crushing the lives of citizens who dared to report law breaking and theft and other kinds of abuse within its various agencies. They were smashing these brave whistleblowers beneath the immense weight of a psychiatric evaluation system that violated the rights of my patients . . . many of whom were being run straight into the "gulag" of forced retirement on a disability pittance that came nowhere close to paying their bills.

Like the Soviet "dissenters" who were routinely being sent to punishment camps (or "gulags") during this same period, the federal employees who came to my USPHS clinic for forced psychiatric exams were the prisoners of a ruthless system of state reprisals that could destroy their lives at will. Suddenly, I began to wonder if the nightmare vision that George Orwell had laid out in his classic dystopian novel, *1984*, might already have arrived in Washington, D.C. – six years ahead of schedule!

Badly rattled, I asked Louie Clark for his advice on the best way to proceed. If the government agency heads were routinely resorting to these illegal tactics to punish whistleblowers, wouldn't they be just as likely to use their corrupt power to punish me for acting in a way that seemed likely to unmask them?

Louie listened carefully to all my questions – and I'm sure he saw the fear in my eyes. "You're gonna have to be careful," he told me calmly at one point. "We're talking about David and Goliath here, and it's pretty clear which one of you is armed with only a slingshot! What I would suggest is that you continue to send your whistleblowers to the news media . . . but do it silently, confidentially, without advertising the fact that you recommended they tell their stories to the press.

"If we can get enough public attention focused on the problem, we may be able to light a fire under some of the leadership on Capitol Hill."

Heartened by Clark's advice, I decided to follow it. During the next few months, with the authorization of the clients, I sent one troubled employee after the next to Indy Badhwar at the Federal Times – after advising each one to say nothing about the source of the information they were offering the press.

Incredibly enough, the strategy actually *worked*. After a few stories about my whistleblowers were published in the Federal Times, a highly regarded Maryland Democratic congresswoman – the late Gladys Spellman, who chaired the House Post Office and Civil Service Committee on Capitol Hill – became increasingly interested in the plight of these abused federal employees.

Finally, Spellman began holding hearings on the problem in her committee. Along with several psychiatrists and well-known mental health professionals from around the country, I testified before her panel and described the forced exams in great detail. How well I remember that cold, blustery morning – February 28, 1978 – when I reported to Rep. Spellman's fifth-floor hearing room in the old Sam Rayburn Congressional Office Building on Independence Avenue. The liaison person accompanied me from the Department of Health, Education, and Welfare to Congress, and this executive had already read my pre-testimony report. His reaction was to suggest that I eliminate the page where I'd made recommendations, since I was not permitted to speak for HEW.

While the House members who made up the Post Office and Civil Service Committee watched intently, I raised my right hand and swore to tell them the "truth and nothing but the truth" about the abuses I was observing daily in the Outpatient Clinic of the U.S. Public Health Service. Then I sat down at the witness table and waited quietly as the Chair began to introduce me.

Mrs. Spellman. *Our next witness is Mr. Donald Soeken, chief psychiatric social worker with the Public Health Service. Mr. Soeken, we are very happy that you could join us today. It is our understanding that you have experience with this system.*

Mr. Soeken. *Yes, I have.*

A moment later, I was leaning forward in my chair and taking a deep breath. This was the first time I had ever appeared before a congressional committee, and my hands shook noticeably as I read through my prepared opening statement.

"Thank you for asking me, Mrs. Spellman.

"This morning I am going to discuss some of my experiences relative to the psychiatric fitness for duty examinations.

"I will first list some of the procedures that we use for the fitness for duty examinations; second, I will discuss the psychological state of the person who is being examined; third, I will describe, in general, the first interview; fourth, I will discuss some of the impressions that come from my experience in using this procedure."

As I read through the document, the hearing room gradually fell silent, until at last the only sound was the sound of my voice going over the statement I had worked so hard to prepare.

"The fitness for duty examination was developed to determine one's fitness to discharge the duties of his job, and is conducted at the request of the employing agency. After an agency complies with all the regulations, an appointment is made by the personnel office of the department requesting the exam. In our clinic, the individual sees a psychiatrist and a psychiatric social worker for an indeterminate number of sessions until the person's emotional condition can be assessed."

After describing the mechanics of the testing process, I went on to point out that the agency employees who take it are usually under enormous psychological stress – since their future careers will depend entirely on the result of one single exam. "A person arriving for such [an exam]," I noted, "is usually in a high state of anxiety. The anxiety might be compared to the kind one might feel after a relative has been in a serious automobile accident and you don't know whether they are going to live or die. . . .

"Difficulties such as headaches, gastrointestinal problems, missing appointments are all common in these cases."

Next I tried to show the committee members how the deck is always stacked against the employee, during these intimidating exams, while explaining: "Under the present system, we have abundant information from the agency's point of view, but a minimum of information from the individual."

While the committee members listened carefully and took detailed notes, I did my best to summarize my opinion of the exams by declaring: "The fitness for duty interview process has a major drawback: When a person comes to the clinic in high stress, he exhibits more anger, hostility and anxiety than a person in low stress."

After that, I pushed hard to make the point that these exams were nothing less than a matter of life and death for the unfortunate souls who were required to take them: "If an individual is judged unfit for duty, as presently constituted, a severe blow to one's vocational life will obviously occur. The time and money necessary to rehabilitate a person after being judged unfit for duty is probably greater than if more intervention was taken before the exam became necessary.

"If a person is judged unfit, he should be given six-month check-ups by a psychiatric team and there should be a genuine attempt at rehabilitation, rather than condemnation by a psychiatric label."

Having completed my opening statement, I did my best to settle back in my chair and relax. But that proved to be impossible, and for good reason: Within a matter of seconds, Mrs. Spellman and several members of her committee had begun bombarding me with some very searching questions.

The chairwoman led off the questioning – and the first thing she wanted to know was whether I believed that the patients who were sent to me should be treated and cared for, rather than grilled by a psychiatrist who was under orders to find out if they could be forcibly retired due to a mental illness.

Mrs. Spellman: "Thank you very much. I get the impression that you and your group seem to attempt to assist the employee rather than to label the employee unfit."

Mr. Soeken: "Yes, I feel that when a person comes with any kind of a difficulty such as this, theoretically I come from the idea that if you increase the stress on an individual, you are going to produce symptoms. And if you can lower the stress, then the symptoms will go to a more acceptable level.

"If we can attempt to lower the stress level by listening to the person, then we can get a pretty good idea as to whether the person is going to take advantage of the help they might get. During the interviews we discuss the person's past therapy and/or counseling, vocational counseling, psychological counseling and if a person has had counseling in the past. We suggest that he start that again, so that we get the symptom level down.

"If you listen to a person long enough, they will get enough of the anxiety out so that they will be more ready to get some kind of assistance . . .. I would like to emphasize that we are not talking, at least the cases we see, we are not talking about serious psychological problems. We are talking about cases that can be helped by therapy, medication, and consultation with the agency."

Mrs. Spellman nodded, and I saw a look of keen understanding cross her face. Her next question, and my answer to it, would make the key point of this hearing – that federal employees were being quizzed by a single psychiatrist during a single exam, even though their careers (and sometimes their very lives) depended on the findings that came out of these brief one-on-one sessions! How could such a one-sided method of interrogation possibly be fair to the employees who were forced to submit to it?

Mrs. Spellman: Are you aware of, or do you know personally of any cases in which employees have been certified for retirement by psychiatrists without a personal examination by the psychiatrist?

Mr. Soeken: "I can't comment on that, I don't think, at this point in time – because I have only seen a limited number of that kind of case, and if I were to comment on that, it would be obvious who I was talking about." [I framed my answer in this way in order to protect the identity of Wilma Jefferson.]

Mrs. Spellman: "I see. I am getting the impression, then, that yes, this is happening, and on the basis of a record that has been compiled by others, a psychiatrist might determine that an employee was not fit for duty."

By the time the hearing ended – on that unforgettable February morning – I was feeling very excited and encouraged . . . because it seemed obvious to me that Congresswoman Spellman and the other members of her committee had *gotten* it: they now understood, clearly and unequivocally, that these forced psychiatric exams were violating the civil rights of the federal employees who were ordered to submit to them.

The ice had been broken at last!

But it took us another five years of ceaseless and unremitting effort... before the Executive Branch of the federal government finally issued a regulation prohibiting the use of the fitness for duty exams as a way of forcing employees into retirement.

In a supremely ironic touch, the new rule was promulgated in the same year that George Orwell had used in his novel to describe the crushing weight of repression in a totalitarian society: *1984*.

Nonetheless, we had won! From that day forward, it would be illegal to punish whistleblowers by making them undergo these psychiatric exams and lose their livelihoods as a result.

But the good news was too late to help Wilma Jefferson. By the late 1970s, she had been forced into retirement on a miniscule monthly disability income of only $300. In addition, the finding of "paranoid schizophrenia" eliminated her chances of ever again finding employment with the federal government. (When I called my former place of employment – the USPHS Mental Health Study Center – and asked if she might find work there, the brass quickly informed me that the mental health diagnosis she'd received instantly "disqualified" her from consideration.)

Although I managed to find her a *pro bono* lawyer who took on her case for no fee, her lawsuit for "wrongful termination" failed to convince a federal judge that she'd been wronged by the Department of Transportation, and she was left to fend for herself, while also caring for a chronically ill child who required expensive treatments and medication.

Of course I was very grateful that we had finally managed to have the fitness for duty exams removed from the arsenal of weapons that federal managers can use against employees they don't like . . . or employees who bravely step forward to speak out against waste, fraud and abuse in their departments.

But whenever I think of the injustice Wilma endured, and of the agonies she must have suffered without a decent income, my blood pressure rises, and I have to resist the temptation to start kicking and shouting with outrage.

If there is any hope in the story of the valiant Wilma Jefferson, it lies in the simple fact that she dared to do the right thing. She was a great hero who put her life on the line in order to tell the truth . . . and she paid an immensely painful price for it. But her actions were not in vain. Thanks to her, the psychiatric fitness for duty exams were brought to the attention of the U.S. Congress, and the practice was abolished.

For that simple fact, all of us owe her a huge debt of gratitude.

In addition, I owe her a second debt. Because of her valorous moral leadership, I became inspired to help whistleblowers by doing my best over the years to provide them with psychological counseling, moral support, temporary housing, legal expert witness help, and a dozen other services that would hopefully make their violent struggles a little bit easier.

Because of Wilma Jefferson and many others like her, I became a specialist in helping whistleblowers to stand tall in the service of truth.

This book is dedicated to Wilma Jefferson . . . and to *all* of those who have faced the ultimate test of whistle-blowing and never faltered in the struggle to live up to the highest ideals and ethics of the United States of America!

TWO

STEVE AGEE – THE HERO IN EXILE

*H*is name is Steve Agee, and although you probably never heard of him, he's actually a great American hero.

A veteran physicist and engineer who told the world about a huge American corporation's allegedly criminal negligence in the Challenger space shuttle disaster of 1986, Agee was a Vietnam combat hero . . . and also a fearless whistleblower who did his best to expose alleged wrongdoing in one of the greatest tragedies of the Space Age. In addition, Agee warned America that she could lose her technological lead and her longtime advantage of holding the military "high ground" on the frontier of outer space.

This is Agee's heartrending story.

They deem him their worst enemy who tells them the truth.
—Plato, *The Republic*

It was snowing again, from Seattle all the way to Utah.

It was the dead of winter in Utah, and it seemed to be always snowing. Steve Agee pulled his stocking snow-cap down over his eyes, hoping to shield them from the windwhipped snowflakes falling on the Great Salt Desert of western Utah.

It was January 1987, and once again a tormented Steve Agee found himself wandering back and forth across the boulderstrewn wastes outside Salt Lake City. A stocky, six-foot-one, powerfully built man, the veteran physicist and engineer knew he had a terrible choice to make – and he knew he'd have to make it within the next 48 hours or so. He was trapped in a dilemma that would deeply affect the entire western world . . . a struggle between American space superiority – once a given – and massive corporate felonies that threatened to *unravel* that superiority, and soon.

Within a couple of days, Agee would have to tell the Federal Bureau of Investigation whether or not he was interested in becoming a "mole" – or "undercover source" – for the FBI.

The FBI wanted him to go undercover at the Morton Thiokol rocket booster plant. They wanted the highly paid engineering consultant to wear a wire, take secret photos, Xerox documents, the works. The FBI brass were convinced they could prove that Morton had violated safety regulations on the manufacture of the space shuttle solid rocket boosters and then lied about it to the U.S. Congress . . . in a cover-up that involved felonies piled upon felonies.

Agee paced. Back and forth he went across the harsh, snowy landscape – a solitary figure in mirror sunglasses who had forgotten how to sleep, forgotten how to eat, so worried was he about the choice that he knew lay immediately ahead. Even worse, he knew there really *wasn't* any choice, morally. For Agee, morality and patriotism had always trumped expediency and safety violations, and this time would be no different.

For nearly a week, Agee had been agonizing over the decision of whether or not to orchestrate a covert surveillance operation deep within the humming, hightech labyrinth that was Morton Thiokol's aerospace manufacturing center, located far out in the desert north of the Great Salt Lake.

Was Steve Agee – the Vietnam combat hero who'd won the Purple Heart – going to stick his neck out for America again?

Or was he going to turn tail and run? Turn the assignment down and "refuse to get involved"? Agee felt anguished about the decision ahead, but there was little doubt about the choice he'd make – because turning and running was simply unthinkable.

He paced. He knocked the snowflakes from his stocking cap. What would happen to Agee if he agreed to go undercover, and then the FBI didn't back him up, didn't protect him fully? It was hard to imagine such a scenario, but you never knew. America's track record on whistle blowers was spotty at best and Agee had always understood: "No good deed goes unpunished."

It was the 14th of January, 1987; at some point during the next few days, Steve Agee knew he'd have to climb into his Toyota Station Wagon for the 40mile run to Salt Lake City, where he would sit down with FBI Special in Charge Agent Robert Bryant and Special Agent Tim Healy and tell them about the decision he had reached.

Was Agee really prepared to take on a multibillion-dollar international conglomerate like Morton Thiokol? A corporation that counted President George Bush, Attorney General Ed Meese and veteran Utah Senator Orrin Hatch among its nearest and dearest friends? It was a shaky prospect, to say the least . . . since Agee had found it increasingly difficult to trust President George H. Bush. He also knew that Meese was under criminal indictment at that point – and that Hatch's reputation for deviousness was well deserved.

Frowning and shaking his head, Agee watched a white jackrabbit go bounding away over the snowcovered rocks. Hell, even a rabbit had enough sense to wear camouflage, and to make damn sure he didn't stand out against the local terrain – political or otherwise.

He paced. He felt his heels crunching into the freshly fallen snow. And slowly, slowly it all came back . . . that extraordinary moment, five days before, when Special Agents Bryant and Healy had eaten dinner with him. During the meal, Bryant had jumped out of his chair and actually shouted, "That's treason!" while referring to numerous issues at Morton Thiokol.

It was a dramatic story, to say the least. A toughasnails Navy Hospital Corpsman who'd been attached to Reconnaissance Marines in the Vietnam War, Agee was accustomed to getting the job done in spite of numbing fear. His story was the story of a true believer – an idealistic kid from the fruit orchards of central California who was accustomed to pushing himself to the limit. As a high school student,

Agee had made outstanding grades – while also winning swimming trophies all across the Golden State as a champion performer on the Mt. Whitney High School Pioneer swim team.

An overachiever from the cradle, Agee had been supremely determined to succeed, after graduation from high school. While working one part-time job after another, he'd put himself through the University of Texas at El Paso on a physics scholarship, earning a degree in Physics and Engineering.

That same attitude had motivated him through 12 agonizing months as a combat medic in Vietnam during the late 1960's. Agee had received seven different citations (including that coveted Purple Heart) for being wounded under fire. Several times, he'd run through gunfire – while the tropical air around him buzzed with AK47 bullets – in order to rescue or perform surgery on fallen comrades.

That was simply Agee's temperament. And it had carried him very far, in only a few years. Having been sent to Morton Thiokol as a top engineering consultant only a few months after the Shuttle disaster in 1986, Agee's assignment was clear. He was to participate in a complete overhaul of the manufacturing giant's Solid Rocket Booster operation, while developing safety and quality-control systems that would prevent future accidents like the one that had wiped out the Challenger and its crew. That accident had also deeply threatened America's space superiority.

Morton Thiokol, aka MTI, was the nation's only manufacturer of large Solid Rocket Motors of the kind that powered the shuttle and military satellites – which meant that the MTI engineers and executives had been responsible for the design and implementation of the failed joints that employed the defective Orings and related components.

After signing on with the Utah corporation and settling into a tiny efficiency apartment in nearby Brigham City, Agee had begun a grueling stretch of 16-hour days, six and sometimes seven days a week. As usual, he was determined to do his job properly. He intended to study MTI's entire operation, and the Space Shuttle operations, from the ground up, and then to let the chips fall where they might. He had no prejudices. He was there at the request of the U.S. Congress and the Rogers Commission on the Challenger Disaster.

And so it began . . . what would become several agonizing months of trying to do the job that the Rogers Commission had tapped him to do – while the execs in the high-rise offices actually did their best to block him and everyone else at every turn.

One of the first such incidents, which set the pattern for all the rest, had taken place just after Agee's arrival. On that particularly nasty afternoon, Agee had asked Kent McKinnon to make him a Xerox copy of Solid Rocket Engineering Safety documents he needed.

But McKinnon had returned emptyhanded.

"It's gone," he told Agee sheepishly.

"Gone?" Agee asked. "How the hell can it be gone?"

McKinnon was staring at the floor. "Nearly [almost] none of the data is going to be made available to you."

"Vanished?" Agee's blood pressure was going ballistic.

McKinnon looked sick. His mouth was white around the edges, and his hands shook. His career was on the line.

Agee just shook his head. "McKinnon," he growled, "you remind me of a saying I used to hear all the time, when I was working down in Texas: 'You can't make chicken salad out of chicken shit!'"

No response. McKinnon just stared helplessly at the floorboards. Agee would eventually write up 244 catastrophic hazard violations. And the team he was on wrote up 1,300-plus. Something would have to be done about these safety lapses, and Agee knew it. Hoping to gain the attention of the Morton Thiokol top brass, he left one message after another for higher managers and McKinnon's immediate bosses.

His calls went unanswered and his requests were evaded.

Furious, he tried to get the attention of somebody higher up in what he had come to call the "corporate food chain".

He got nowhere.

"They're treatin' us like yesterday's cat shit!" the colorful Agee would thunder, while sad-sack McKinnon hung his head.

In the end, Agee decided to call on the FBI. Having held various security clearances for years, he and the Bureau enjoyed a mutually symbiotic relationship. But it took him three days to make arrangements to call the FBI from a "clean phone" near the MTI plant.

But at last he came face to face with an FBI agent, who calmly measured his visitor and then said: "I am Tim Healy, Special Agent, FBI, and here are my credentials." Then the big man's face creased into a friendly smile. That was the beginning of a relationship that continues to this day- 25 years later.

In the end, Healy and Agee talked for more than three hours—during which Agee described the dozens of safety violations he'd witnessed during his months on the job at Morton Thiokol. He also described how MTI had been refusing to fix anything. He handed over documents to prove his points.

When the long catalogue of abuses had fully unfolded, Healy gave a low whistle. "Steve, if this stuff is true, we're talking about a conspiracy to lie to NASA, the U.S. Congress, and the Rogers Commission."

Agee nodded.

"Exactly."

Healy chuckled. "That's right. Okay, let's say you go back to work tomorrow, like nothing has happened. Let's say you continue to make your rounds, but keep a low profile. Just do your paperwork, file your reports – the sameold sameold. Then, nearly every night, you can be debriefed by one of us. And all the while, you'll be working for us. You'll be taking some pictures and Xeroxing some files . . . maybe wear a wire and try to collect some commentary from MTI officials about the Oring problem and other problems."

Agee agreed.

Green pennies . . . he could taste them again. The taste of green pennies in his mouth. That was fear, of course. It was pretty ironic, really – the way Agee had assumed his career would be full of proud accomplishments, and not the fear he'd felt in combat.

Hadn't he left fear behind on the battlefields of Vietnam?

"Contact! Contact! Hit the dirt!"

They were several miles northwest of Dong Ha in the I-Corps – another roundtheclock Recon Patrol – when the Viet Cong mortars suddenly began to open up. The soldiers went face-down in the jungle, and Agee went with them. He lay silent against the earth, a 23year-old kid from small-town California, listening to the hollow whump . . . whump . . . as the shells exploded over their position and the bullets snapped by.

Each time a round went off, they could hear the shrapnel whistling through the tangled jungle that flanked the trail.

Green pennies in your mouth.

Agee had been a champion athlete – a top high school swimmer – and he thought he'd learned how to handle pressure, during all those nosetonose battles with powerhouse competitors in the 200yard breast stroke and the 400yard individual medley. But this was different. This was off the charts. He listened to the highpitched, droning whistle of another arriving Chinese mortar . . . whump! . . . and again the taste of green pennies flooded his mouth. This was not win or lose, it was life or death.

"Man down! Man down! Corpsman . . . Andrus is down! Where the fuck ARE you, Agee?"

Agee hesitated for a moment. Green pennies . . . and his heart was racing, pounding furiously in his chest. Would he be able to handle the load? Could he face up to the test that lay ahead right then?

A moment later, he was on his feet . . . racing down the trail, oblivious to the danger of a bullet, the everpresent threat of a Punji pit. He found Andrus stretched out beneath a Banyan Cypress, one of those huge trees with the knobby roots . . . only these roots were streaked with red, bright scarlet. They were smeared with Andrus' blood.

"Hey, doc," said Andrus. His voice was no louder than a whisper.

"It's okay," said Agee. "It's okay, Andrus, I'm here." His hands had gone to the medical kit. His hands were shaking. Absorbent Bandage, sulfurpack, morphine . . . He looked over and his heart sank: Andrus' abdomen had been torn open. Agee could see his organs through the torn muscle above Andrus' ripped entrails.

"I'm cold," said Andrus. "Steve . . . I'm c-c-c-old."

"It's all right." Agee started to work. He could see the light dimming, already dimming, in Andrus' shellshocked eyes.

"Doc . . . are they gonna get me out? Will they get me out in time?" Andrus made a gurgling sound; his mouth was crawling with scarlet bubbles. Steve could taste the green pennies. He kept tasting the green pennies, and he would taste them for the rest of his life.

Andrus' life ended there. Many lives would end in front of Agee.

The light was out. Andrus' eyes were open, wide open, but they were sightless.

The light had died.

Green pennies in your mouth . . .

⟨⎯⟩

Steve Agee, American hero.

Here is what the U.S. Federal Bureau of Investigation had to say about Agee's decision to report the alleged crimes at MTI, during the months that led up to the Challenger disaster, as reported in an official U.S. government document obtained under the Freedom of Information Act:

> U.S. DEPARTMENT OF JUSTICE
> FEDERAL BUREAU OF INVESTIGATION
> Salt Lake City, Utah
> Nov. 13, 1989

NOT TO BE CIRCULATED

"On January 17, 1987, a system safety engineer, STEVEN AGEE, employed at Morton Thiokol (MTI) as a consultant, contacted the FBI regarding alleged criminal violations by MTI officials. He alleged that MTI officials lied to the President's Commission which was formed to investigate the Challenger accident. He also claimed that MTI was falsifying data to NASA, and that employees from MTI used strong-armed tactics to discourage employees from providing information to the Commission.

"AGEE was employed by MTI through ARC, a Phoenix-based contract engineering company, responding to the U.S. Congress to provide engineering consultants to MTI and many others. AGEE provided tremendous amounts of documentation to support his claims. He also introduced the investigating agent [Healy] to several MTI engineers, systems safety engineers, and managers to support his allegations. Some of these people were converted into FBI sources."

One of the first witnesses that Agent Healy interviewed would be System Safety Supervisor McKinnon. Had Agee been telling the truth about McKinnon and McKinnon's refusal to confront the company brass over its safety lapses, and MTI's alleged conspiracy to lie to the federal investigators about the cause of the accident? Healy answered that question as follows:

NOT TO BE CIRCULATED

"MCKINNON was interviewed and acknowledged that his job had been threatened if he came forward with safety concerns during the presentation.

"Based on MCKINNON'S letters and statement, and the interviews of the witnesses, it appears that MTI intended to provide false statements or withhold information to the Government."

P acing.
Back and forth Steve Agee went, while the snow slanted into the Azul Mesa and the elk roamed over the table-rock. If he took the plunge – if he agreed to put his entire life on the line for the Bureau, and for the U.S. Department of Justice – would they back him to the limit?

Or would they hang him out to dry, if and when the political pressure from well-connected MTI really took off? What if MTI knew how to get to Ronald Reagan, or Ed Meese?

Agee believed that every person has a cross to bear and has to face the moment of truth.

For Steve Agee, there had never really been any doubt.

Semper Fidelis.

By God, he was U.S. Navy and U.S. Marine Corps! He would do his duty. He would wear the wire, and he would Xerox the critical documents. He would do his best to give the FBI what it needed, in order to proceed with criminal indictments.

At last he turned away from the mighty, snowcapped vista of the mountains . . . turned back and walked through the snow toward his waiting Toyota wagon and the 27mile drive back to Brigham City.

He would take the plunge.

He would call Special Agent Healy, first thing in the morning.

A s he climbed behind the wheel, on that fateful afternoon in January of 1987, he could taste them in his mouth.

Green pennies . . .

Steve Agee, the Vietnam War hero, knew what was coming.

Was it Socrates, 2,000 years ago, who had summed it all up in a single, unforgettable phrase?

"Most of all, they hate the man who tells them the truth. . . ."

COUNSELING A WHISTLEBLOWER: WHAT IT'S LIKE

I woke up with the first ring of the telephone.

Blinking slowly in the dark, I waited for my mind to clear. Then I glanced toward the illuminated hands on the clock at the bedside table.

They read: *3:07.*

And that could mean only one thing: One of my struggling whistle-blowers was in trouble tonight.

Still half-asleep, I fumbled for the receiver. As my hand touched the cool plastic, I felt a wave of gathering dread. It was the usual syndrome: icy fingers, a swirling breathlessness, and the taste of sour metal in my mouth.

Call it "intuition" – a sixth sense that usually warns me when a whistleblower is about to plunge off the track and career toward a devastating catastrophe.

"Don? Are you there?" The voice on the other end of the line shook badly. I could hear the stress in it. I could feel the stress arcing into my dimly lit bedroom in Maryland, all the way from far-off Australia. "Don, it's me – Steve Agee."

"Hi, Steve. Yeah, I'm right here."

"Sorry to wake you up, man, but I was climbing the walls. I was scared shitless, and I didn't know where else to turn."

"That's okay, Steve. What's the problem, exactly?"

"They're following me again, Don. *Them*. And they were tailing Fay all afternoon today, even to the supermarket. Our phone calls are diddled [intercepted] and our mail is redirected. And two guys attacked me in a parking lot. I beat the shit out of them and left. I'm unclear if it's MTI or the U.S. Government, and I'm very stressed!"

I thought for a moment. "Easy, Steve. Take a deep breath. It can't last much longer, you know that."

He barked with sudden laughter . . . but then the laugh turned into hacking cough. "I bought another gun, a .357 Magnum. And Fay kept saying: 'I won't live this way. I won't live in a world where the father of my children has to carry a weapon!' I don't blame her, either. That's why she insisted we leave the U.S. in the first place – to get away from all the guns.

"Can you believe we've been living in Australia for more than a year now? I've left my country, my work, my security clearances and I'm marooned in Australia."

I was rubbing my eyes. "I'll talk to her, Steve. I'll calm her down, don't worry. Why don't you try to get some rest?"

He sighed. "Who can rest? Let's face the facts, Don. Okay? The cat is out of the bag, know what I mean? They're *onto* me because a DOJ attorney published the fact that the FBI had sources inside MTI. They know I talked to the Linkage Supervisor, and they know he spilled his guts. They also know I've heard the tape of what happened in the Command Module, right after the O-Rings gave out.

"They know I heard the part where the astronauts are mostly cursing and blaming Morton Thiokol –"

His voice broke, and all at once I was listening to a tormented man who knew there was no place to hide on Planet Earth. The DOJ and the FBI had failed him.

"Don . . . what I'm wondering now is . . . do you think they know I wore a wire for the Bureau? Do they know I spied on them for the U.S. Government?" At that point, it seemed certain to him that they did know.

I thought about it for a moment. The bedside clock ticked softly in the background . . . and then I heard the gentle patter of summer rain against the window. "Probably not, Steve," I lied. "And besides . . . even if they *did* discover that you were working undercover at Thiokol, they wouldn't dare take on the Feds.

"Nobody wants to go one-on-one with the FBI."

He coughed again; it was the deep, growling cough of a man who smoked two packs of unfiltered Camels each day. "You always say that," he groaned now. "You always say that they won't mess with the Bureau. But is it true? I mean, don't you think they're pretty desperate by now . . . given the fact that they're trying to cover up their actual role in the Challenger disaster?

"The fact is that MTI had no qualms about going head to head with the FBI. After all, they had Ed Meese, the U.S. Attorney General, on their side!"

He was silent then. Frowning and alarmed, I began hunting for the words that might comfort him. But they were nowhere to be found. To be honest, I was no longer certain that the FBI *could* protect Steve Agee from the faceless corporate bureaucrats who ran Morton Thiokol – or from the gun-wielding thugs who allegedly did their bidding out on the street. What could I tell him? For at least half a minute, I sat there speechless on the edge of the bed, while a ghastly newspaper headline drifted through my tangled memory:

WORLD WATCHES SEVEN DIE
AS SPACE SHUTTLE EXPLODES

At last I opened my mouth to speak, but the deeply rattled Agee beat me to the punch.

"Don, I wanted to let you know . . . I'll be flying into Washington from Perth tomorrow afternoon."

I nodded. "That's great news, Steve. We can meet at the Irish Pub in Laurel. What did you call it, the last time you and I met there? The best little Irish pub in America? I'll sit you down over a soda, and maybe things will start to make more sense."

He laughed . . . and then he began to cough. "Sounds real good, Don. God knows I need to loosen up and relax. The crimes I've uncovered will cost the taxpayers billions of dollars."

I was smiling now on my end. The Irish Pub was a priceless resource, in my line of work. Tucked away on a back street in suburban Washington, D.C., the popular Irish watering hole never failed to soothe my depressed whistleblowers . . . most of whom would light up happily, once you put a cold soda in their hands. I'd taken Agee there twice before for strategy-planning sessions, and he'd fallen deeply in love with the joint.

"I can't wait to shake your hand, Don. And listen . . . I'm gonna bring along a couple of documents I Xeroxed last time I was inside the Thiokol plant. Okay? They're engineering specs, and you aren't gonna believe your eyes when you see what they have to say about the O-rings."

I nodded. "I hear you, Steve. And I'm eager to see what you've got. But I want you to get some rest, okay?"

"I'll do my best."

"Okay. Try not to worry. I'll see you tomorrow night."

"You bet, Don. Can't wait."

"Good night, Steve."

I returned the phone to its cradle. Then I stretched out again in the darkness of the shuttered bedroom. But sleep wouldn't come. I lay there, glassy-eyed and staring, while the clock ticked on and on, while it snipped off the seconds like a pair of scissors working endlessly inside my overheated mind. . . .

STEVE AGEE AND MORTON THIOKOL: DAVID CONFRONTS GOLIATH?

More and more these days, I found that I was becoming afraid of my own job . . . as a Licensed Clinical Social Worker who specialized in providing psychological guidance and vocational advice to some of the nation's most high-profile (and most deeply troubled) whistleblowers, including FBI, CIA, NSA, DOD just to mention a few.

After more than a decade of counseling courageous truth-tellers like Steve Agee – the physicist-engineer who'd told the world about Morton Thiokol's criminal negligence in the Challenger space shuttle disaster of 1986 – I was finding it increasingly difficult to witness the emotional agony that these brave whistleblowers were so often required to endure.

Steve Agee was a blunt, no-nonsense professional who'd "gone public" with his reports of incredible safety lapses at the huge corporation in Utah, soon after the catastrophe. And he'd been punished quickly as a result. First he'd been fired from his job at MTI. Then he'd been "blackballed" by the industry, harassed by private detectives and finally even assaulted by two thugs on an Australian parking lot . . . triggering a blood-soaked fistfight that had required overnight hospitalization for the two who attacked him. But Agee dared not tell his wife about the incident, or mention the fact that the two assailants had been severely injured – and that Agee was concerned about being arrested by Australian authorities.

Recruited by the post-disaster Rogers Commission as a rocket expert who might be able to shed light on the causes of the in-flight explosion, Agee had gone far beyond the call of duty in helping America to understand what had gone wrong. At one point, in fact, he'd even volunteered to "wear a wire" for the FBI, while working deep inside the company's main rocket plant in rural Utah. Those recordings had been passed on to the FBI under a judge's authorization.

Acting with incredible bravery, Agee had photocopied thousands of potentially incriminating documents inside the plant. Then he'd tucked them inside the waistband of his suit trousers . . . and had brazenly carried them past Thiokol Security, before handing them over to the FBI on a nightly basis.

But Agee's valiant heroism had gone for naught.

In the end, after he'd risked his life to help the Feds build a massive criminal case against the rocket-maker, Agee had simply been "dumped" by President George H. Bush's administration. Indeed, there was now compelling evidence to show that powerful members of that administration had intervened to muzzle the FBI probe . . . to the point that Agee's FBI "handler" had finally felt obligated to warn him: "Steve, we can't protect you any longer. You better get yourself a piece. Better yet, get the hell out of the country before somebody tries to whack you."

What a nightmare.

As a veteran mental health counselor who specializes in the problems so often encountered by whistleblowers, I'd been doing my best to help the nerve-shattered Steve Agee for the past two years. But I hadn't been able to do him much good. Increasingly isolated and frightened, he'd finally taken off for Australia with his family . . . where he was now hunkered down, powerless and penniless and fighting a losing battle to win compensation in the U.S. court system for the illegal Thiokol firing that had wrecked his life. In Australia Agee was "tall popeyed" and couldn't find any appropriate meaningful work.

Why had the brass at the aeronautics firm kicked Agee out into the cold? According to Agee, this was because they were all corrupt.

The answer was simple enough: the Big Dogs at the corporation – along with their powerful cronies on Pennsylvania Avenue and at NASA – wanted their controversial former consultant to come apart at the seams. They wanted him to send up a white flag . . . to give up his lawsuit against MIT before something was said in a courtroom that would open a window on their own responsibility as the manufacturers of the SRB's and the O-rings that had triggered the catastrophe.

And now Steve Agee was on his way back to the States.

He was scheduled to spend at least a week giving depositions in Washington, while also tending to a dozen other chores related to his "wrongful termination" lawsuit.

Exhausted and out of financial resources, Agee was a man trembling on the brink. Somehow, I had to find a way to help him survive this ruthless onslaught from corporate America . . . an all-out assault, backed up by the immense power of the U.S. political establishment, that now threatened to erase him from the annals of whistle-blowing.

How could I help Steve most?

Still sleepless, I watched the rain tapping gently against the window-glass for a while. I closed my eyes and listened to the peaceful drumming of a summer shower in the nation's capital, and to the gentle breeze sighing against the eaves of the house. But it was no good: sleep would not come.

There was no cure for it except to climb out of bed and pad down the carpeted hallway in my bare feet toward the study where I kept all of my whistleblower case files.

Stretching and groaning, I flicked on an overhead lamp.

A moment later, I was pulling the thick AGEE file from the file cabinet in the far corner of my office. And then I went straight to work, determined to help him in every way I possibly could.

But my efforts fell short in the end, and Agee paid a huge price for his courage and his faithfulness.

The following January, Agee was totally destroyed, after a California attorney filed a $36 million lawsuit against MTI for the whistleblower, and also a Qui Tam lawsuit for the American Government that sought to recover billions. But a DOJ lawyer who was crucial to the case refused to get off his backside in order to pursue the suit effectively. His excuse was that NASA had "no contract" due to its own sloppiness. In the courtroom, Agee and his attorney were literally "jerked around." It was an obscene display of orchestrated injustice from beginning to end, he says today.

Then, after Agee had been destroyed in the USA, he emigrated to Australia, where the harassment and the problems continued. The abuse was so bad that an Australian company called Titus Films Production eventually made a documentary about the case, entitled "Nice Guys Finish Last." The documentary was ultimately shown on television all over the world, usually via public TV.

Agee lost millions of dollars in the wreckage that followed. He lost his career momentum and his security clearances, and he ultimately lost his marriage and his three children by that marriage. Yet he turned out to be correct on every single issue, and, per his predictions to the FBI, the USA eventually ended up without a Space Shuttle or even a viable rocket to power it.

After Agee's marriage disintegrated, he moved on to New Zealand and then traveled back and forth to Washington D.C. In Washington, he managed to reacquire the security clearances, and he helped develop emergency plans for the U.S. Federal Reserve Bank, which was a major contribution to helping protect the U.S. economy. He wrote the startup logic for the FBI's Internet Fraud and Complaint Center and then he was called back from New Zealand to orchestrate the new FBI TSC (Terrorist Screening Center). All were successful new program/organizations.

Today Steve Agee lives on a remote beach in New Zealand. He is very ill and he lives alone. He says that his severe health problems were brought on by his attempt to blow the whistle on the shoddy engineering and manufacturing processes that were in large part responsible for the loss of seven brave astronauts.

"I don't know what's become of this country," Steve told me just the other day, during a long-distance phone call from his tiny village on the other side of the world.

"This isn't the same country I fought for in Vietnam. This isn't the America I have always loved. What are we going to do if we lose our sense of trust in each other, and in the Constitution which we all vowed to defend?"

Listening to him, I just shook my head.

THREE

Linda Lewis Takes On the Federal Government

– By Herself

I t was raining again.

Perched behind the wheel of her silver-blue Geo Prizm, Linda Lewis watched the busy rush-hour traffic zooming past on the other side of her windshield. It was after five p.m. – and already getting dark – on the chilly afternoon of November 3, 1997.

Linda was in terrible trouble.

And now, as she drove north on the Baltimore-Washington Parkway, only a few miles from the nation's capital, the realization had begun to sink in.

High-level government officials reportedly were very upset with her. Why? It was quite simple, really.

Linda, a federal government employee, had committed an unpardonable sin.

Alarmed by what she felt were dangerous gaps in preparedness to protect the citizenry from radiation in the event of a major leak at a nuclear power plant, the 47-year-old Lewis had contacted staffers in the office of U.S. Senator Joseph Biden—the soft-spoken and easygoing senator from Delaware who would one day become the Vice President of the United States. Twice, Lewis had telephoned and sent faxes, in

September and October 1997, asking for Biden's help in dealing with a crisis of management in the Radiological Emergency Preparedness (REP) program.

Lewis's message to Senator Biden was urgent and it was crystal-clear: Don't believe what FEMA is telling you about the results of last year's Delaware Radiological Exercise!

Deeply disturbed by the eleventh-hour phone call, Senator Biden apparently made a few phone calls of his own . . . and it was soon obvious to the brass at USDA that the "whistleblower" who'd alerted the senator to the looming danger at a nuclear plant was none other than their own Emergency Planning Specialist, a meddlesome stickler for honesty named Linda Lewis.

As Lewis would later point out during an interview for this book: "The problems I reported to Sen. Biden involved inadequacies in Delaware's preparedness to protect the food supply from contamination by radiation in the event of a disaster at the Salem Nuclear Power Plant. The problems were covered up by the Region III office of the Federal Emergency Management Agency (FEMA). The REP program provided oversight of state and local preparedness for radiological emergencies. FEMA administered the program and other federal agencies, including USDA, contributed staff to assist with training, plan reviews and evaluate emergency exercises.

"According to FEMA's formal report, the Salem exercise, held October 22-25, 1996, had been a smashing success...and state officials had effectively demonstrated the ability to protect the public from contamination by radiation in a nuclear plant disaster. In fact, multiple problems had been identified by evaluators, including me.

"In my evaluation report, I had documented the failure of Delaware state officials to properly identify boundaries around the area declared 'contaminated.' As a result, other agencies did not know where to establish 'access control points' where uniformed responders would be posted to prevent 'contaminated' farm produce and retail foods from being shipped out and sold to unwary consumers. Notably, inadequate access control led to widespread concerns in Japan about the safety of the food supply following the 2011 Fukushima Daiichi nuclear plant disaster.

"The FEMA exercise leader reviewed and initially approved my findings, but state officials – who had bullied me and withheld evidence – demanded a perfect report. The exercise leader caved, telling evaluators that all of the problems we reported would be excluded from the official report."

As an Emergency Programs Specialist experience on the Emergency Planning Staff in USDA's Food Safety and Inspection Service (FSIS) since 1992, Linda knew that, under federal law, USDA had a duty to ensure that the food supply would be protected from contamination in the event of a nuclear, chemical weapons, or other emergency. "I objected immediately to the planned whitewash," she said later. "But, as a GS-13 USDA employee, I had no authority to stop it. I reported the whitewash to my supervisor and tried going up the chain of command to achieve some kind of resolution of the problem, but to no avail. FEMA responded by trying to blacklist me from Region III activities."

Then, in September, 1997, Lewis says, she discovered a frightening fact: the controversial nuclear power plant had been brought back online after a two-year shutdown caused by major safety problems. Senator Biden, she learned, had requested an investigation by the Government Accounting Office. In fact, the Salem reactors had been deactivated by the federal government because of maintenance problems that threatened to cause a possible meltdown. During the shutdown, investigators had discovered such problems as a leaky generator and defective reactor controls.

Alarmed by the very real possibility of a "radiological disaster" in the mid-Atlantic region, Lewis decided that she had no choice but to notify Senator Joe Biden about the false reporting at the last Salem exercise.

"Salem had been a very troubled nuclear plant in the mid-1990s," Linda recalls today, "and now they were going to restart it. In that case, they would need to have good emergency plans in place. Morally and ethically speaking, I knew I had an obligation to protect the public in case of leakage or meltdown problem that could have put their lives at risk."

Ask Linda Lewis how she gradually woke up to the fact that FEMA was routinely deceiving the public about nuclear preparedness, and the now-retired, 62-year-old civil servant won't mince her words. "It was a gradual awakening," she said during a series of recent interviews in which she described how her professional career was destroyed due to her whistle-blowing. "I think I realized very slowly, one inkling at a time, that deceptiveness and fraud were woven into the way we did our business.

"I think that this kind of slowly increasing awareness is often what happens with whistleblowers. You start out with a suspicion that problems are being papered over, but there's no conclusive evidence that wrongdoing has occurred or that the public is endangered. Then, you witness something so clearly reprehensible that it compels you to act."

And now, as she piloted her car along the highway that led to her small apartment in the Washington suburb of Odenton, Maryland, Lewis was remembering the meeting she'd had with her boss, only two hours before.

"Sit down, Linda. There's something we need to discuss."

Nervously, she had settled into a chair. She sensed she was about to receive some bad news, but was not prepared for what her boss said next.

"I understand from a discussion with some of my colleagues that you contacted a certain senator a couple of weeks ago. Is that correct?"

For a few seconds, Linda sat in stunned silence. No one in Sen. Biden's office had ever contacted her after receiving her communications, and she had assumed that the disclosures had been tossed in a "circular file."

"Yes. I did make that call," she said, finally.

"Your letter upset some very important people. Why did you send it?"

"I was deeply concerned that flaws exposed during the last exercise were ignored. In my judgment, FEMA's failure to report them correctly puts the people of Delaware at risk in the event of a nuclear plant accident – and it is our job to protect them, isn't it?"

He nodded. He frowned. A moment later, he was on his feet. "I'm going to discuss this incident with my supervisors. I doubt that you will ever again evaluate an exercise in FEMA Region III." End of discussion. Period.

Was it also the end of her career? Linda wondered. She had read about Peter James Atherton, a Navy man and nuclear engineer at Maine Yankee Nuclear Plant. He had reported safety issues, but his superiors had done nothing to correct them. So he tried to take his concerns to President Carter, himself a nuclear engineer. The Secret Service called Atherton's bosses, then had Atherton forcibly admitted to St. Elizabeth's for a psychiatric evaluation. He was eventually vindicated and Maine Yankee was shut down, but his career had been destroyed.

Linda Lewis had taken a huge risk. Alone, she had decided to blow the whistle on an abusive practice at a major federal agency.

RETALIATION

"I hoped that my bosses would not react like Mr. Atherton's," she says today. "But, by Thanksgiving, it became clear that my supervisors were trying to fabricate an excuse to fire me, often with help from their subordinates. I would be falsely accused of emotional outbursts on duty and forced to refute the claims. Witnesses who praised my work and demeanor as professional, even exemplary, were threatened, harassed, fired, or simply ignored. In the months that followed, I was subjected to a steady stream of threats, verbal assaults and humiliation. I was denied access to needed resources, and those in control of my travel arrangements, repeatedly left me with no rental car or hotel room."

"It was stressful knowing that traps were being laid for me and that I had to perform perfectly, no matter what. Still, I managed to keep my emotions under control while on duty. Off-duty, however, I frequently cried, sometimes for hours. It seemed to relieve the accumulated stress of the day... at least until the next morning when the harassment would begin again."

On May 5-7, 1998, the largest nuclear emergency exercise in U.S. history was conducted for the Salem plant. Both New Jersey and Delaware participated, along with an army of federal officials. Described by press releases as "nearly two years in the planning," this was a remarkable event. Normally, an ingestion pathway exercise was held every six years, but not even two years had passed since Delaware's last—the 1996 debacle. The official explanation was that the feds wished to "develop a national model for the integration of federal, state, and local plans." Was it also a vindication of Linda's concerns? Or just a bigger whitewash?

"I can't say—I wasn't invited," says Linda. "But it's interesting that the official report for the October 1996 exercise disappeared from FEMA's website."

The harassment was worsening, and, by summer's end, Linda felt so threatened and marginalized that she was desperate to find a new job. "I managed to land a temporary assignment in a new branch of the USDA that was charged with determining the equivalency of foreign food inspection systems to ours. I went to my new job in a hopeful spirit . . . but it wasn't long before I realized that there were some disturbing anomalies in our foreign meat inspection program. . . ."

Yes, you guessed it.

Within six months of joining the foreign equivalency branch of FSIS, Linda Lewis would once again become embroiled in an exhausting struggle to tell the world about deceit, fraud and cover-up inside the federal government.

"I was assigned several countries and immediately noticed that the country files were in terrible shape. Misfiles were common, because many documents had not been translated by the firm under contract to do that."

"One day, the unit supervisor called me to inquire about the status of Panama's application. Meat imports from Panama had been banned since 1984, and Panama needed to file a plan for detecting drug residues. Much of the documentation was in technical Spanish, so I asked the supervisor to allow a translator to review the file. To my surprise, she denied my request. Then, she pressured me to confirm that Panama had met equivalency requirements. I explained that I couldn't know that until the file was translated. The supervisor repeated her demand – again and again. The pressure was intense, but I refused to draw any conclusions about material I could not read."

Failing to enforce U.S. food safety laws could open the door to contamination, not only by residues of toxic chemicals but also by diseases such as bovine spongiform encephalopathy (aka "Mad Cow Disease"). In June 2000, USDA's Inspector General would slam the equivalency program's managers for playing fast and loose with equivalency requirements – while also relying on inadequate documentation to grant equivalency status to six countries. But, on February 8, the investigators were still collecting evidence, and Linda's bosses were escorting her out of USDA. They kept her on paid administrative leave for a week, then ordered her to return to "work" at her new "office"—a closet inside a room used to store surplus and broken furniture awaiting removal. For weeks, she received no assignments.

Then, in mid April, Linda received a letter notifying her that her "Top Secret" security clearance had been suspended. The letter ordered her to take a mental status exam in order to keep her job and regain her clearance, but did not explain why USDA considered Lewis a security risk, except to vaguely allege the existence of negative information.

A few months earlier, USDA had ordered a "reinvestigation" of Linda's clearance. A government investigator then interviewed several mental health professionals who had treated Linda for depression, and all told him Linda had no condition that would preclude her from having a clearance. Without explanation, a mysterious reviewer labeled the endorsements as "negative" information.

A FRANTIC PLEA FOR HELP

Realizing that she needed expert advice, Linda telephoned me for help in April 1999. The first thing I did was to sit down with her and ask her to tell me her life story. I listened carefully to her description of her early life as a child in Cincinnati, and to her stories about her courageous father, Timothy Lewis, a World War II veteran who'd served valiantly in a tank battalion in northern Italy.

Linda began college with the expectation of becoming an investigative journalist, but later switched her major to geology. She earned a degree in geo-science from the University of Texas at Dallas in 1979, and worked for awhile as a geoscientist. When geo-science jobs dried up, Linda took a temporary job as an emergency dispatcher. That's when she discovered a passion for helping people in crisis. She began studying for a degree in emergency management at the University of North Texas, the only U.S. college then offering it. When Linda graduated in 1989, she became one of a handful of people in the world with that degree.

As soon as I heard about her upbringing – and especially about her childhood in a strict Lutheran family where religious piety and truth-telling were valued above all other virtues – I knew that Linda "fit the paradigm" of the typical whistleblower. Again and again over the years, I've discovered that people who blow the whistle are almost invariably the products of deeply religious and ethical families in which their conduct was expected to be absolutely above reproach. And that was certainly Linda Lewis: an intelligent woman with a deep commitment to honesty and public service.

I also understood, of course, that she would be severely tested as a result of her decision to speak out against the wrongdoing she had observed at the U.S. Department of Agriculture. During many years of counseling courageous patriots like Linda, I had compiled a long list of the chronic problems that typically follow in the wake of whistle-blowing . . . problems that can include everything from economic destitution (after jobs and related employee benefits are lost forever) to devastating clinical depression, to disabling anxiety, to broken marriages, alcoholism and even suicide attempts in some cases. Make no mistake: as my research has demonstrated frequently over the years, blowing the whistle on waste, fraud and abuse in government and business can be extremely hazardous to your health!

Because the impact of speaking out against wrongdoing can be so paralyzing, I've often advised people who are contemplating such a move to "slow down, settle back, take a deep breath" – and then think long and hard about what they hope to accomplish by "going public" with their charges of abuses in government or business or industry. Above all, I tell them, it's extremely important that a whistle-blower should *never act on impulse* . . . but only after a lengthy, thoughtful review of all the possible consequences of "telling it like it is"!

In Linda's case, the price to be paid for telling the truth about the flawed "Radiological Exercise" in Delaware was surely going to be very high. Based on my earlier research (including a key 1988 psychological study involving 230 whistleblowers that had been reported in the New York *Times*), the odds were very much against her. My research data had shown that people who shared her type of background – high achievers from ethical families where attending religious services was supremely important – were statistically doomed to suffer overwhelming pangs of remorse and anxiety, along with intense feelings of persecution, once their bosses set about the task of delivering reprisals for the whistle-blowing.

As I listened to Linda's history, I found myself wincing in anticipation of the agonies I knew she would face. All her life, she had been an "overachiever"–racking up straight A's in college and earning the respect of peers in her profession.

When I asked Linda to describe the "attitude" she usually took toward her job and how she went about doing it, this nervy whistleblower didn't pull her punches. "I admit that I'm a perfectionist, Dr. Soeken," she told me. "I take my oath as a federal employee very seriously, and I'm determined to do my best to accomplish our mission – which is to protect the American people from the effects of a disaster.

"I frequently take work home with me at night or work late at the office on assignments that I feel require extra attention. I care deeply that we *get it right* . . . and when I learned that we weren't doing that, and that we were actually 'doctoring the results' of some of these exercises in order to deceive the public and Congress about our ability to protect them in an emergency, I was totally devastated. I couldn't believe that the management at the USDA would stand for such deceptive practices, and I knew that I would have to speak out against the practice, regardless of the consequences."

Listening to Linda describe what happened next, I just shook my head.

After more than two decades of counseling truth-tellers like her, I knew what was coming, as she began to describe the "reprisals" and the "punishment" and the "payback" that she began to endure within days of calling Joe Biden's office to report wrongdoing at the mighty USDA.

PAYING THE "ULTIMATE PRICE"

As I watched Linda's case unfold, I witnessed most of the devastating symptoms that so often attack whistleblowers who dare to put their lives on the line – depression, anxiety and crying.

Like most of the whistleblowers I've known over the past three decades, Linda Lewis was willing to pay a very high price for her refusal to assist in the emergency preparedness cover-up by the USDA and FEMA. Within two weeks of her phone call to the U.S. Senate, she was already being punished for her temerity.

The brass at the USDA wanted her out of their hair . . . and their hired guns from the USDA/FSIS Personnel Office (along with a platoon of psychiatrists who were sure to "find" whatever mental ailment was required of them) would do their utmost to declare Lewis mentally incompetent and thus end her career by taking away her security clearance.

But I was equally determined to *prevent* that. The battle for Linda Lewis' career was about to be joined – and I quickly decided that it would not be fought in silence. With my Rolodex at the ready, I was prepared to call every print and TV news reporter I knew in Washington.

THE BATTLE

By May of 1999, I would be working many hours to help Linda with her case. This included recruiting a partially pro bono lawyer who would assist her with "wrongful termination" issues and volunteering to sit in on the forced psychiatric fitness for duty exam that her bosses were requiring of her. (Because Lewis had been issued a national security clearance, she could be compelled to take the exam. Her security clearance meant she was still vulnerable to fitness for duty testing – even though we'd managed to eliminate the test for most of the nation's 2.5 million federal employees, way back in 1984.)

Having counseled hundreds of whistle-blowers during the 1980s and 1990s, I knew that the turning point in Linda's case would come when she took her psychiatric fitness exam. I informed her that although she would be required to take a psychiatric fitness for duty exam in order to keep her security clearance, she was *also* entitled under federal law to take the test from a psychiatrist or psychologist of her own choosing.

I spoke with USDA's Chief Medical Officer, a physician. He was the USDA official designated to decide whether Linda's mental status justified restoring her clearance. He agreed with me that, instead of sending Linda to one of USDA's "hired guns," it would be better to review the findings of professionals who had seen Linda over an extensive period of time.

After reviewing my report and letters from a psychiatrist and a psychologist who had treated Linda for depression, the Chief Medical Officer agreed that she was not mentally ill and wrote a June 1 memo recommending restoration of her clearance. This did not sit well with his superiors, who were not physicians. They falsely claimed the law prevented him from accepting the findings of Linda's healthcare providers and pushed him to rescind his memo, which he ultimately did.

Meanwhile, Linda was still trying to do her job. She had been given limited duties that included reviewing draft emergency plans prepared by inexperienced USDA employees. The plans were inadequate to ensure continuity of operations or protect USDA facilities and workers in a terrorist attack, Linda concluded. She arranged for an FBI terrorism expert and a FEMA expert on writing emergency plans to brief the USDA planning team, tentatively on July 28. But senior managers angrily cancelled the briefing, Linda learned, and the harassment intensified.

A week into September, Linda's supervisor handed her a letter placing her on paid administrative leave and again ordering her to have a mental status exam, and only by a USDA contractor. Two appointments were set up in October with a psychologist who, Linda says, told her it would be unethical to base a mental evaluation on allegations from her coworkers. Nevertheless, the psychologist was briefed by one of Linda's chief harassers and reviewed a USDA "smear file" that excluded evidence supporting Linda's claims of harassment.

Hoping to minimize the impact of an exam in which her career would be on the line, I requested that I at least be allowed to sit in on the proceedings. I hand delivered the report I had done to the psychologist who was doing Linda's exam. I was not allowed in the exam room, but the message was delivered that if "you do not conduct a fair exam, the whole world will be watching and they will know the results of your unethical exam."

The psychologist had Linda complete a multiple-choice personality test. At the second appointment, "The psychologist said the test results were all normal," Linda told me later. The psychologist sent USDA a report dated November 5.

On December 2, Sen. Barbara Mikulski sent a letter to USDA requesting a response to Linda's concerns. Five days later, FSIS contacted its psychologist and prompted her to expand on her conclusions. The psychologist responded with a December 13 letter alleging that Linda had a "paranoid personality disorder."

Since there was never any evidence that Linda had a "paranoid" disorder, however, it was clear that someone in personnel had requested that a letter include the words "paranoid personality disorder". None of Linda's therapists or examiners had ever concluded that she had such a disorder. In fact, this was simply their method for neutralizing her efforts and destroying her credibility.

What had happened was that the personnel officer had gone around the Chief Medical Officer of the USDA in order to lay the groundwork for a medical exam that was completely bogus. The USDA hired a psychologist who completely ignored Linda's attempts to explore her concerns as a whistleblower. The psychologist ignored my report and did not refer to it as evidence supporting Linda's contention that she was mentally stable and healthy.

In a "smoking gun" email dated January 7, 2000, an FSIS official cited Sen. Mikulski's letter and Linda's "whistleblower allegations." The same email noted that "the Department" had revoked Linda Lewis' security clearance that day. But the fact was that only USDA's Chief Medical Officer had the authority to review the psychologist's report and decide if it justified revoking Linda's clearance *and he never even saw that report* as he said later in a deposition. In short, FSIS and USDA officials had orchestrated a complete end run around their own Medical Officer.

Linda remained on administrative leave for months. Then, just before Christmas, 2000, USDA threatened to fire her in 30 days. I quickly found an attorney for Linda to help her respond to the threat. In addition, I arranged for a reporter to interview Linda about the problems she had reported. That reporter called several of the officials involved and questioned them in detail about the apparent reprisals against Lewis. After a tense 30 days, the USDA officials blinked. They did not carry out their planned threat – but they didn't withdraw it, either. They simply left it dangling like a sword of Damocles over Linda's head.

Lewis was still on forced leave on September 11, 2001, when terrorists hijacked American Airlines Flight 77 and plunged it into the Pentagon—located just across the river from USDA's offices in Washington, D.C. As smoke billowed from the Pentagon, rumors spread of attacks on other federal buildings. USDA headquarters was in chaos – exactly what Linda had tried to prevent. But, the situation was worse at another USDA office… located in Tower 6 of the World Trade Center, now ablaze. Agencies and the American Red Cross called staff and volunteers to respond to the horrific scene at the Pentagon. In a strange twist of fate, one of those who got the call that day was the same psychologist who had stopped cold Linda's efforts to prepare the government for terrorist attacks.

Suddenly, it seemed that Ms. Lewis could read the future. Nevertheless, it took two more years of legal wrangling before USDA allowed Linda to report to work. After a due-process-free "hearing" of Linda's appeal of the revocation of her clearance, USDA conceded that her duties didn't require a clearance, after all. In January 2003 – after three and half years on administrative leave at taxpayer expense – Linda received a fax telling her to return to work.

RETIRED NOW – BUT SHE WILL NOT BE FORGOTTEN

In October 2005, Linda reached the minimum retirement age of 55. "I hated to leave," she says, "but I knew I couldn't take it anymore. I was struggling with chronic physical illness, worsened by stress, following exposure to unexplained chemical fumes in my office. I filed for immediate regular retirement and two years later was granted a disability pension that would give me 40 percent of my salary."

Several times earlier that year, Linda had warned FEMA and USDA officials that FEMA's procedures for coordinating federal disaster assistance were too bureaucratic. She noted that they could result in federal agencies "standing idly by" while overwhelmed local authorities failed to protect human lives.

A few weeks after Linda's last warning, Hurricane Katrina devastated New Orleans. Tens of thousands of hurricane victims were left helpless for weeks, in what still ranks as one of the most embarrassing and disgraceful performance failures in the history of the federal government. FEMA officials were lambasted by local government leaders in Louisiana, Mississippi and Alabama for their utter inability to coordinate disaster relief.

A year later, Linda was living in a tiny apartment and watching her pennies, having retired on a USDA pension. "I lost my career and I never have enough money, these days," she told me a while ago. "It wasn't fair, yet I feel fortunate. On the Gulf Coast, 1,800 people paid with their lives and thousands more lost their homes, jobs and communities because the government wasn't prepared for Katrina. What happened to them wasn't fair, either."

As a veteran counselor to whistleblowers, I wasn't surprised to learn how Linda's story ended. Again and again over the years, I've seen how the reprisals by angry company bosses and bureaucrats almost invariably ruin the lives of courageous Americans who dare to stand up against waste, fraud and abuse.

Although she fared better than most – she's still alive, and she's still got a roof over her head – I don't think there's any doubt that Linda Lewis paid a high price for her willingness to tell the truth and thus protect the citizenry from the kind of nightmare that occurred in New Orleans on August 29, 2005.

Today she lives in a modest duplex apartment in Hagerstown, Maryland, having been driven out of the Washington D.C. area by the high cost of rents. She still struggles with illness. Yet she has often insisted on volunteering to help other whistle-blowers like herself, and I've sent more than a few of them to her in recent years. She settled her case against USDA out of court in 2009, so that she could devote time to her ill father, who was dying of cancer. He died in 2009 – after telling her on many different occasions how "proud" he was of her whistle-blowing.

In the past, Linda Lewis' story would probably never have been told – she would have vanished into the maw of history without having received any recognition for the self-sacrificing heroism she clearly displayed. But that didn't happen, in this case. Thanks to her daring selflessness and her insistence on upholding the highest ideals of the federal government, I was inspired to write this book – and to tell her brave story, along with the stories of many other bold whistle-blowers like her in recent years.

Linda Lewis will not be forgotten; the memory of her valorous struggle will live on, far down into the future!

FOUR

A Truth-Teller for Our Time

F red Whitehurst Risks Everything To Expose Corruption At The FBI....

Prelude

Fifteen years after his titanic struggles as a whistleblower who dared to charge the Federal Bureau of Investigation with wholesale fraud and misconduct in the explosives evidence laboratory where he worked as a Supervisory Special Agent and expert scientist, Dr. Frederic Whitehurst would write a thrilling autobiography in which he tried to explain how his father's shining example had inspired him to risk everything in order to protect America from rampant corruption at the FBI.

Never published, that autobiography would begin with a stirring depiction of how Whitehurst's father – a super-patriotic naval officer named William Burgess Whitehurst – had often been forced to leave his beloved family behind in the Navy towns where he was stationed . . . while serving as the commander of a destroyer that prowled the Pacific in order to help defend the people of the United States.

The name of that destroyer was the *USS Brush*. And each time she set sail from a Navy pier in California for another six-month odyssey on the high seas, the youthful Whitehurst and his mother and his three brothers would stand at the end of the pier and watch the ship pull slowly out to sea.

Huddled together, they would grieve at the prospect of the long, empty months that lay ahead – months in which they would be deprived of a deeply loving and deeply committed father.

But they also understood why he had to go – and they would not have dreamed of calling him back.

"My daddy loved his country deeply," says Fred Whitehurst today. "He was a patriotic man, and he was an *honest* man. He called a spade a spade . . . and he insisted on living up to the highest ethical standards in his own conduct as a military officer."

As he watched from the Navy pier, Whitehurst vowed that he, too, would someday devote himself to the service of his country.

He did so . . . but not in a way that he could have ever imagined.

"When my time came to confront the fraud and the perjury and the deceit that was routinely taking place at the FBI, it was my father's image that loomed before me," Whitehurst recalls today. "And it was his legacy of service and loyalty that I knew I had to honor in every choice I made."

How important was Fred Whitehurst's officer-father in shaping the values that would eventually inspire his son to become one of America's most controversial – and most famous – government whistleblowers?

To answer that question, all you have to do is read the first chapter in Fred's unpublished autobiography, which begins as follows:

> ***The impressions that first stand out in my mind about my childhood are about sacrifice and pride. My father was a naval officer. That meant we lost him often to the sea and duty to the nation. Having come from a harshly poor background, my father had the strength to follow his convictions over far horizons in the face of high seas and stormy weather. And following his convictions he taught us about sacrifice and the pride we have as Americans living in a free society.***

I remember most clearly the horizon. We stood on the sea wall on the coast of California in the middle 1950s as my father's ship disappeared over the horizon. There was always a horizon. We were four brothers and my mother, alone, losing my father again and again to his loyalty to our country. I remember so clearly the tiny ships on the horizon, so far away they seemed like little toys, with stacks smoking as they moved out of sight. And I remember knowing that Dad was not coming home tonight or for many nights to come, many months to come, almost as if he had died for a while. I remember my mother, without tears though we knew she was crying inside, keeping us so busy around the house in those first few weeks after my father would go off to sea or to duty overseas. It was her way of chasing away the loneliness and starting us to look forward to the homecoming, to the joy of sacrifice.

And I remember very clearly seeing my father walk down a gangway from his destroyer on his return from one of those voyages. He was proud, his back straight, a stern look on his face, there from the weight of the responsibility of the lives of men serving on his ship. I remember as if it were yesterday my mother bending down to my ear and telling me to look at the way my father walked, with his back straight, his head high. I would walk like that also, she said. I would walk with a straight back in life as I also faced high seas and stormy weather.

A FRIGHTENING FIRST ENCOUNTER

Meeting Frederic Whitehurst for the first time was a nerve-wracking experience that I won't soon forget.

During my thirty years as a psychological counselor who specializes in helping whistleblowers, I've worked with some very tough people . . . many of whom were at the breaking point and on the edge of total nervous collapse. I've counseled high-ranking corporate executives who were crawling with paranoia, and I've tried to help Pentagon whistleblowers who were convinced they were being wire-tapped by "dark-side operatives" during every waking moment of their lives.

But nothing could have prepared me for Fred Whitehurst.

I first met Fred on a blustery winter afternoon in early 1993, while he was the supervisor of the Evidentiary Explosives Lab at the FBI and was struggling to pick up the pieces of his shattered life.

"Dr. Soeken, you gotta help me," he'd told me on the phone a few days before this introductory session. "I'm running up against some very hard-nosed folks at the Bureau, and I really think they're trying to do me in. I've had the brakes fail twice – for no apparent reason – on my brand-new Ford. I've been getting threatening messages on my home phone and in the mail.

"I think the pressure is starting to wear on me, and I'm not sure how much more I can take. How soon can I meet with you to discuss my case?"

Feeling more than a little uneasy, I took a long, hard look at the man sitting across from me. Then I stared at the bulge along his belt. For a moment, I felt a twinge of stark fear: *What if he snaps completely during the session and decides to pull out that gun? What then?*

Although I was reassured by the fact that Whitehurst had compiled an excellent record at the FBI – his performance reviews had produced nothing but "Outstanding" scores for many years – I was a bit dismayed to learn that he had volunteered for three back-to-back tours of combat duty as an infantryman and later in military intelligence at the height of the Vietnam War. Whitehurst had earned not one but *four* bronze stars (along with an Army Commendation Medal) for his service – although he has always insisted: "I was not a war hero, but just a simple soldier doing my job."

I knew Fred had been an outstanding soldier – and I also knew that his reputation for selfless valor reached all the way back to 1965, when he'd been awarded a Navy Marine Corps Medal for Heroism after rescuing a drowning man trapped in a car at the bottom of an icy pond. Only 17 years old at the time, Whitehurst had displayed an astonishing amount of personal courage in risking his life to save the struggling victim. Again and again, he'd dived 12 feet deep into the frigid water in a desperate effort to pull two people out of the submerged car.

"I went right in, navy overcoat, shoes and all," he would write years later, recalling that life and death struggle at the bottom of the winter pond. "As I broke ice, the water felt warm underneath relative to the air. I swam with the overcoat and shoes on out to the car. The top was just above the water, but, as I reached the car, it sunk below the surface. I dove down and pushed into the driver's side window. I saw a face, a man come out. I helped him out, and we surfaced.

"At first he was disoriented, but then, as I yelled at him, he and I began to swim to shore. 'Is there anyone else in the car?' I kept asking him. Halfway to the shore, he yelled that a kid was in the car. A child. A child was in the car. I swam back. Back at the car, I went under again and again, three times. The car was in about twelve feet of water, totally submerged at that time, resting on the bottom. On the fourth time I went under I saw what was actually a man, struggling to free himself from the inside. I reached in and pulled him out and got behind him. We surfaced with me holding onto him from behind. . . . "

Whitehurst does not like to be referred to as a hero, however, and I've often heard him say: "I'm just a simple, ordinary American who tries to help other people when I see they need it. I think most people would do what I have done."

As I thought about his life-story, however, and about his remarkable adventures, I just kept on shaking my head in amazement. Here was a man who clearly deserved the title of "larger than life." But this was also a man who readily admitted to feeling deeply depressed at times. How would he react when I began questioning him about his "state of mind" as a whistleblower who was now being harassed and punished for daring to tell the truth about the fraud that was taking place almost daily in his FBI crime lab?

"I know you've been through a lot, Fred," I told him as soon as we sat down on that bone-chilling winter afternoon in 1993. "I also understand that talking about your experiences as an FBI agent may be difficult for you."

He nodded grimly at me. "You're right, Don. This is the toughest thing I've ever done, by far. I thought Vietnam combat was difficult – but fighting Charlie and the North Vietnamese was a cakewalk, compared to facing the devastation I've been through lately, ever since I decided to blow the whistle on the perjury and the fraudulent test results we were routinely turning out in my laboratory."

Now he leaned in closer. His eyes were huge, and they were burning with pain. I was feeling a little better by now, since he seemed calm and reasonable. "I never thought I'd see the day when my own country would try to destroy me," he said at last. His voice was low, almost a whisper. "Even now, a year after they fired me and threatened to put me in jail, it's hard to believe that all of this happened.

"Quite truthfully, there are days when I almost doubt my own memory . . . when I wonder if all of this really happened. But it did. I've got the files; I've got their correspondence; I've got taped interviews with the brass that show clearly how they set out to annihilate me after I went public with my testimony about the fraud and the perjury they were committing in the lab daily, in order to convict people in the courtroom."

I nodded. "Take your time, Fred. Try to relax. Don't try to hurry it up in order to get to the ending. Just let the story flow out of you at its own speed."

He gave me a thumbs-up sign, and then sent me his jumbo-sized, trademark grin. "Okay, Don, I hear you loud and clear. Here goes!"

RIGHT FROM THE START, HE REFUSED TO LIE

Fred Whitehurst was 34 years old on the day he joined the FBI in 1982 – a deeply idealistic Special Agent who was determined to give his all to the country he loved.

For the hard-charging Whitehurst, becoming a fabled "G-Man" was a dream come true . . . a chance to follow in the patriotic footsteps of the Naval officer-father whom he had so deeply admired.

But that dream would be flawed, right from the start.

On the morning he first reported to the Bureau's massive headquarters building in downtown Washington, Fred climbed into a cab in front of the hotel where the FBI had lodged him for the night. Although he didn't know it at that moment, he was actually only a block or so away from the crime-stopper agency's headquarters. But he made the out-of-towner's mistake of telling the cabbie that he was new in Washington and about to begin his first day on a brand-new job.

The cabbie responded by driving him around the city for half an hour and then charging him $11 for what was only a one-block ride. "It was a symbolic moment," Whitehurst says today, with an unhappy shake of his head. "I was cheated on the way to my first shift at the FBI . . . and as soon as I walked into the building, I learned that the Bureau *also* wanted me to cheat on the job!"

It happened only an hour or so into the day, when Whitehurst was told by his brand-new supervisor that he should note on his attendance sheet that he'd arrived for work at 7 a.m.

Reacting with shocked disbelief, Whitehurst reminded the supervisor that he hadn't actually arrived until 8:30, his scheduled starting time. The supervisor frowned and told him: "Fred, we *always* sign in at 7 a.m. That way, you're sure to rack up a lot of overtime during the week. It's part of the drill here, that's all. If you don't do it, you'll make the rest of us look bad!"

Years later, the disillusioned Whitehurst would sigh unhappily as he recalled the moment when the scales began to fall from his eyes. "I signed it . . . but I didn't like it, because I'd been taught as a boy growing up that you didn't lie. And it hurt like hell to learn that the FBI was cheating the citizenry like that."

It didn't take Whitehurst long to come up with an ingenious solution to the problem, however.

"After a few days on the job, I realized that if I came in early every morning, I could sign in at 7 a.m. and my attendance sheet would be in accord with the facts.

"From then on, I always came to work at 5:45. It cost me a little bit of sleep, but I felt a whole lot better as a result."

For the moment, at least, Fred Whitehurst had found a way to reconcile his powerful sense of right and wrong with the cynical reality he confronted inside the FBI.

Unfortunately, however, his struggles with the "culture of deceit" that he would find everywhere inside the massive federal agency were only beginning. And within a few years, the conflict between Whitehurst's ethical sensitivity and the bureaucratic hypocrisy he hated would erupt in a violent struggle that would end up on the front pages of newspapers all across America.

DISCOVERING "PERJURY" INSIDE AN FBI CRIME LAB

He was an outstanding FBI agent; even his sharpest critics in the Bureau will readily admit that much.

During his first few years as a Special agent, Whitehurst nailed down one "Outstanding" performance review after another.

The Bureau acknowledged as much in 1986 . . . by detailing him to become one of its top technicians at the FBI Explosives Evidence Laboratory in Washington, D.C. With a chemistry Ph.D. from prestigious Duke University in his back pocket, Whitehurst was a logical choice to work in the high-tech crime lab. Meticulous and diligent, he was also a perfectionist who insisted that the rules of evidence-gathering and analysis should always be observed down to the last detail.

Soon after arriving on the scene in Washington, Whitehurst found himself assigned to a high-profile mentor, a veteran chemical analyst and evidence-gatherer. Whitehurst was eager to begin learning his craft as a chemist whose job was to sniff out often-microscopic traces of high-powered "accelerants" . . . including exotic plastic explosives and other explosive ordnance that was being used by some of the world's most sophisticated and deadly terrorists.

At first, things seemed to go well. But as the months passed and Whitehurst spent long hours working beside his FBI mentor, he became increasingly disturbed by the things he was seeing. Amazed and alarmed, he noticed that his boss frequently failed to run required clean-up procedures in the lab . . . a major breach of protocol that could easily lead to "contamination" of evidence, if even minuscule quantities of explosive powders or liquids were left on assay tools or lab surfaces between laboratory shifts.

Never a shy violet, Whitehurst was quick to challenge his new boss' failures at cleanup and maintenance. But his complaints fell on deaf ears, as his new boss impatiently waved him away and mocked his "perfectionist" insistence that they follow lab regulations carefully.

The cleanup failures were bad enough. But they seemed almost trivial, a few months later, when Whitehurst discovered that his boss was breaking another cardinal rule by "working backwards" from the criminal allegations against suspects to the evidence itself.

The "backwards" transgressions were a way of saving time and energy for the lab technicians . . . by having them look exclusively for any evidence that might successfully convict a suspect in the courtroom – while ignoring anything that might tend to exonerate the suspect.

"Working backwards" was a profound and dangerous violation of crime lab evidence-gathering standards . . . since it could easily lead to the most egregious betrayal of justice imaginable: the false conviction of a suspect, who might then wind up serving years in prison for a crime that he or she had never committed.

Horrified to discover that the FBI lab crew frequently used the "backwards" approach in order to lighten their workload, Whitehurst soon realized that the rule-breaking lab workers were also willing to "doctor" their results now and then, if it made life a little bit easier for the FBI agents and the DOJ prosecutors more likely to win an important crime conviction.

Once again, Fred Whitehurst felt disillusioned and betrayed. How could his beloved Federal Bureau of Investigation stoop to this kind of prosecutorial fraud? How could they knowingly provide tainted evidence that might convince judges and juries to destroy the lives of people who might be innocent?

"That was a very hard time for me," Whitehurst recalls today. "No sooner did I arrive at the lab in Washington than I was assigned to someone who right away started teaching me the art of perjury.

"Well, I know I wasn't going to be able to tolerate it, that's all. I took a long hard look at what they were doing, and I just told myself: 'I'm not going to stand for this. I'm not going to put up with it.'

"On more than one occasion, I'd stood up against war crimes while serving in combat in Vietnam. I'd been in situations where I refused to allow people to be tortured, refused to allow VC prisoners to be executed. And I felt the same way about the perjury that was taking place in the FBI lab. Somehow, I knew I would have to find a way to stop the fraud and enforce the rule of law at the FBI."

A SHOWDOWN AT THE COURTHOUSE

When the showdown finally came – in the summer of 1989 in San Francisco – it triggered a violent and protracted struggle that would convulse the entire Bureau, all the way up to the office of FBI Director Louis J. Freeh in Washington.

The battle between Fred Whitehurst and the FBI began in earnest during the trial of a businessman named Steven Psinakis, who had been charged with secretly gathering explosives for shipment to the Philippines, where they were allegedly going to be used in an assassination attempt against longtime Philippine dictator Ferdinand Marcos. As was often the case, the U.S. Department of Justice was depending on evidence from the FBI explosives lab and one of longtime top analyst to deliver the key testimony that would convict the reported arms dealer.

But as the controversial trial got underway in the federal courthouse in the City by the Bay, Whitehurst was having some very painful second thoughts. "At that point, I knew from my own on-site inspections that the evidence that would be presenting in court was useless," the disillusioned chemist would later tell me. "The lab was filthy dirty at that point, and the truth was that the agent had screwed up the analysis from top to bottom.

"This wasn't just a situation where a few details were out of place. When I reviewed the lab notes and his top-to-bottom report on the case, my heart sank. Virtually everything he had put together was deeply flawed . . . and it was quickly apparent to me that we couldn't proceed to trial with it.

"The evidence we were going to present to the jury was essentially meaningless – and when I examined my conscience, I saw that I just couldn't be a party to the misrepresentation that was about to take place."

Tormented by doubts and uncertainty, Whitehurst remembers "walking around San Francisco all day long. I was upset as hell," he says today, "because I knew what would happen if we showed up in court with that kind of garbage. Would we help to convict an innocent man? What was my moral and ethical responsibility [in such a] complicated situation?"

At one point, Whitehurst remembers standing in front of a historical marker near Fisherman's Wharf and reading a bronze plaque that described how hundreds of thousands of men had shipped out to fight in the Pacific during World War II from that very spot. "I was crying," he recalls, "and the tears were just running down my face. And I kept asking myself over and over again: 'Is this why they died – so that we could take the idea of justice and the rule of law . . . the idea of freedom for all from tyranny . . . just take those great American values and flush them down the commode?'"

No!

"I decided . . . by God, I would not be part of it – no matter how much it cost me!"

In a flash, Whitehurst understood what had to be done. Retracing his steps to the courthouse, he marched inside and began looking for an expert chemist named Lloyd Snyder, the key "expert witness" for the defense team that was representing Steve Psinakis.

One can only imagine the shock and amazement Dr. Snyder must have felt, when Whitehurst rushed up to him with an urgent request: Could they talk together about the FBI lab report that was about to unveil in the courtroom?

Once the two men were alone together, Whitehurst blurted it all out. "Dr. Snyder . . . I know it may surprise you to hear this, but I'm convinced that my partner intends to lie on the stand. He's going to testify that he found chemical evidence of explosives on the materials that were taken from the defendant's office . . . but I can tell you for a fact that his analysis is deeply flawed and it doesn't say a damn thing about whether or not the traces of accelerants he studied were actually from explosives ever in the possession of Steve Psinakis!"

Stunned to the teeth, Dr. Snyder thanked the FBI analyst for his courage and honesty . . . and then hurried off to confer with the defense team. And the results? As you might expect, Steve Psinakis was ultimately found innocent of all charges in the case.

Whitehurst was not so lucky, however.

Although the Assistant U.S. Attorney who'd been handling the case for the government ultimately wrote a letter to FBI Director Louis J. Freeh stating that he had reviewed the entire matter in detail, and that he was convinced Whitehurst had "done the right thing" in revealing his doubts about the mangled evidence, it was too late to save the Vietnam war hero from the retaliation that followed.

Whitehurst had "crossed the Rubicon" with his decision to blow the whistle on the malfunctioning explosives lab, and there was no turning back.

Within a few days, his life at the FBI would become a "living hell" – a brutal nightmare in which enraged agents and supervisors up and down the chain of command would do their best to punish him for having gone public with his information about the fraud and the perjury that he had witnessed daily in the FBI lab.

PUTTING HIS LIFE ON THE LINE . . . FOR FREEDOM

During the months that followed Whitehurst's ethics showdown in San Francisco, life in the explosives lab became almost unbearable, as the besieged truth-teller was reviled endlessly by his office mates and by angry executives in the FBI chain of command. Increasingly, Whitehurst found himself being treated with disdain and outright hostility by his colleagues. Deeply frustrated and disillusioned by the retaliation, he nonetheless somehow managed to keep his cool.

"The reprisals were really brutal at times," he remembers today, while describing how his spouse Cheryl – a longtime FBI employee herself – was also harassed and intimidated constantly during the first few years after he went public with his observations during the Psinakis trial. "It got so bad that Cheryl started waking up at 1:30 in the morning, night after night, and just puking her guts up. It hurt me like hell to see what they were doing to both of us . . . but especially to her. Honest to God, I don't know how I managed to survive some of those days."

He hung on as best he could, however, while working hard to keep his job performance at the highest possible level. Amazingly, his employee evaluations during this stressful period – performance reviews that were assembled yearly by FBI Case Supervisor James Corby – remained consistently "Outstanding."

"Jim Corby saved my life," notes Whitehurst. "In spite of the fact that the FBI brass was doing its best to shut me down, he had the courage to write honest evaluations of my on-the-job performance during the early 1990s. That showed a lot of integrity and honesty on his part, and I owe him a debt that can never be repaid. He acted in a way that was consistent with the highest ideals of the Federal Bureau of Investigation."

During February of 1993, as Whitehurst continued to hold on by the skin of his teeth, the Bureau finally came up with a strategy that seemed likely to dislodge the whistleblower from his shaky perch and send him into early retirement. The name of that strategy was "forced fitness for duty psychiatric exam," and the notice was dated February 19, 1993. According to the FBI communiqué he received that day, Whitehurst was to proceed immediately to Chicago, where he would be interviewed at length by both a psychologist and a psychiatrist – both of whom were contract employees of the Bureau.

He called me immediately. "Don, what's happening? Do I have to submit to these tests or what? The whole thing is rigged – they're going to declare that I'm crazy and then use that diagnosis to boot me out of my job. Can you help?"

I could. Within an hour, I was on the phone to the employee counseling office, and was reminding them that Fred Whitehurst had come to me to be examined by his *own* psychological expert, if the Bureau really wanted to get a reading on his state of mind. What followed was a month-long feeling of fear . . . in which I worried that the Bureau might take me into court to prove that I was incompetent to counsel this whistleblower . . . and that it certainly *did* have the legal right to demand he submit to testing by their in-house psychiatric crew.

In the end, however, it was the Bureau that blinked. With the help of his attorneys, after many hours of discussion, the FBI decided that Whitehurst could indeed obtain his own psychological counseling if he paid for it. And it didn't take me long to find overwhelming evidence for the obvious: Fred Whitehurst wasn't schizophrenic, or manic-depressive, and he didn't have a character disorder. Nor was he "clinically depressed."

He was excitable (who wouldn't be, given the vocational pressure he'd been under for many years), and he was prone to outbursts of temper at times . . . but my interviews established beyond a reasonable doubt that he was in very good psychological health. Indeed, as I wrote after a phone conversation with the employee counseling service: "Fred Whitehurst is completely fit for duty, by any reasonable standard that one could apply. There's nothing wrong with him – he's just a highly ethical person!"

After continuing to blow the whistle and fighting retaliation, including being placed on administrative leave in 1997, he eventually retired early from service in Washington to take up his present occupation as a criminal lawyer in small-town North Carolina. By then it was clear that he'd won his battle with the Bureau and had prevailed as a special agent whose integrity had never been impugned.

Indeed, the United States Office of the Inspector General (OIG) would provide a ringing endorsement of Whitehurst's service to the FBI in 1997, in a report that noted for the record:

"Whitehurst justifiably raised concerns within the Laboratory about his partner's work habits, and Whitehurst's persistence on this issue ultimately resulted in the FBI directing a review of all of the other agent's cases.

"Similarly, Whitehurst correctly complained that EU [FBI Explosives Unit] examiners in certain cases have testified outside their expertise or issued opinions that are not scientifically supportable, the World Trade, Avianca, and Oklahoma City cases being prominent examples. . . .

"We recognize also that Whitehurst's complaints have resulted in both internal reviews within the FBI and this OIG investigation, and thereby may have helped achieve changes that will enhance the objectivity and reliability of the Laboratory's forensic work, particularly in explosives-related cases."

Now in his sixties, Fred Whitehurst lives in the tiny community of Bethel, N.C., where he works daily to protect the rights of defendants in criminal trials. He also serves as the director of the National Whistleblowers Center's Forensic Justice Project – where he continues to advocate for national reforms in the standards of evidence and laboratory procedures related to criminal prosecutions.

Ask Fred Whitehurst why he risked everything for the sake of cleaning up the mess at the FBI labs, and this valiant whistleblower will tell you about a man named Donald Eugene Gates – a man who spent 28 years in prison after being convicted (on the basis of tainted FBI evidence) of a rape and murder he did not commit. As NBC News reported on the day the falsely convicted Gates was released from prison (Dec. 15, 2009): "The conviction was based largely on the testimony of an FBI forensic analyst whose work later came under fire and a hair analysis technique that has been discredited."

Says Whitehurst: "That was a terrible miscarriage of justice, and it happened because the FBI lied. And if they had been able to shut me down – if they had succeeded in silencing the whistle-blowing that I was determined to achieve – Gates would have probably stayed in prison until the day of his death.

"But that didn't happen. He is free today, and the Constitutional guarantees that rescued him are also alive and well in the America of 2010.

"But the survival of our freedoms in this country is by no means guaranteed. It depends on the willingness of every one of us to stand up against fraud and waste and abuse in high places – and it *absolutely* depends on our willingness to help protect the whistleblowers who put their lives on the line to keep those freedoms intact!"

FIVE

BETRAYAL

This is the story of a man who loved the Marine Corps so much that he did the unthinkable: He blew the whistle on his Marine superiors – by testifying before the U.S. Congress and tipping off the major U.S. news media to a tragic scandal at the headquarters of the USMC. He became a whistleblower . . . with predictably painful consequences that continue to echo through his turbulent life today.

FRANZ GAYL THE MARINE

Ask Franz Gayl to tell you what he thinks of the United States Marine Corps, and this proud veteran will light up brighter than Yankee Stadium during a night game.

"I enlisted in the Marines on my seventeenth birthday, way back in 1974," Gayl says today, "and the Corps became my life. It was and remains my heart and soul. The Marine Corps put me through college and then through graduate school, twice. Everything I am now, I owe to them. As far as I'm concerned, the ideal of the Marine Corps motto 'Semper Fidelis' says it all."

As Gayl points out, that Latin motto – when translated into English – means: "Always Faithful."

Franz Gayl spent over 22 years in uniform as a faithful member of the USMC. Like all enlisted Marines, Gayl completed three months of "boot camp," then continued with another two months of Infantry Training School, or "ITS". At the end of about six months, he was a full-fledged infantry Marine: an "anti-tank assault-man" to be precise. Within a year he was sent to Marine Security Guard (MSG) School and with a newly investigated and approved top secret clearance was stationed as an Embassy Guard in Germany. Following a three-year tour he was honorably discharged as a sergeant, and remained in Germany to work as a bodyguard for the CEO of a major German multinational.

Later he returned to attend college in Minnesota. Missing the Marines, he rejoined, and, after attending Officer Candidate School and college graduation, he was commissioned as a Marine officer. He became an infantry officer. In addition to deployments, he attended Army Airborne, Ranger and other professional Schools. He also served as a tactics instructor and later commanded a Weapons Company. The Marines also sent him to graduate school, where he received a Master's degree in Space Systems Operations. After a Pentagon tour, he retired at the rank of Major, and in 2002 was immediately rehired as a civilian science and technology advisor, at the civilian rank of GS-15, the equivalency of a full bird Colonel. Later he was assigned to an internship at the renowned Defense Advanced Research Projects Agency (DARPA), and then attended and received a second master's degree from the National Defense University.

"There were times when I had to pinch myself," he remembers today, while describing his startling odyssey from high school drop-out, to Marine Corps Sergeant, to USMC Major, and then technology-savvy weapons and equipment analyst.

"Over my 38 adult years as a Marine, my youth has become unrecognizable. I have discovered that I had abilities inside me that I'd never dreamed of. I can hardly believe my good fortune."

But beginning in the fall of 2006, his charmed life would be changed forever.

Immediately following his second graduate school stint, the idealistic Gayl voluntarily deployed to Iraq at the invitation of the senior

Marine general in Iraq, who had once been his supervisor at the Pentagon. There he served as the science advisor to the forward deployed I Marine Expeditionary Force (I MEF) in Al Anbar Province.

THE TRAGIC AND UNNECESSARY LOSSES IN AL ANBAR

It was the late summer of 2006, in the heart of Anbar Province at Camp Fallujah, a large forward operating base some miles outside the city of Fallujah and the still-violent Ramadi. Day after day, and night after night, the Marines had been taking casualties, all across the restive Al Anbar province. Sometimes the losses were caused by skilled snipers, and at other times by the downing of helicopters, by small arms fire, or by unguided rocket and mortar fire. More often than not, however, the casualties were caused by anti-vehicular Improvised Explosive Devices (IEDs) – jerry-rigged explosives assembled by a growing cadre of technologically savvy Iraqi insurgents – that were buried beneath and beside roadways.

Upon his arrival at the I MEF Forward HQ, Franz Gayl was told by his new superiors of the threats, and of the bureaucratic obstacles that Quantico officials appeared to be employing to slow and stop the delivery of equipment solutions. Gayl's task was to help "accelerate the speed and quality of the Corps' support establishment response" to counter the cruel and clever insurgency that was raging in theater. Gayl was well aware that the technological and commercial solutions for many of these threats were readily available, given a collective will to field them quickly.

It was a routine sight to observe a CH-46 or other transport helicopter arrive with the overhead escort and cover of a single Cobra gunship. Invariably the passengers included one or more critically wounded Marines or Soldiers who had been struck by an IED. Their destination was Fallujah Surgical, a field hospital aboard the base that routinely performed heroic feats in successfully treating trauma that in any previous conflict would certainly have proven fatal. Calls went out for this or that blood type to replenish supplies. Confined to a desk where he wrote requirements, Gayl felt operationally useless, but routinely giving blood at the hospital helped ease his bad conscience. Of course many of the wounded could not be saved. One early High Mobility Multi-Purpose Wheeled Vehicle (HMMWV) IED death impressed him deeply.

"That was one of the worst feelings I think I've ever experienced. I mean, we just stood there after we learned the worst about one familiar Marine. I knew in the back of my head from what I was encountering that so many tragedies including this one were unnecessary. And it wasn't because of an act of enemy ingenuity, a freak of nature, or even political resistance. No, it was because our Marine Corps support establishment for whatever reason didn't do its job of delivering the capabilities that were needed to take care of their own."

It was clear that what he was learning and experiencing in Al Anbar had changed him forever. "Day after day, I received the reports of Marines killed and maimed because they lacked proper weapons and equipment. HMMWV death traps were the biggest concern, but gaps in the realm of Intelligence, Surveillance, and Reconnaissance (ISR) systems like unmanned aerial systems and ground cameras proved equally deadly. All of these gaps could have been filled with commercial systems and delivered within weeks. But those deliveries were apparently being consciously obstructed. As I witnessed the tragic consequences first hand, I suspected that it was a knowing corruption of the support process that was taking place, not just errors and misunderstandings."

Confirmation came quickly. During his tour, Gayl learned from others that the Marines in the field had urgently requested, but were then deprived of, easily obtainable "Mine Resistant Ambush Protected (MRAP)" vehicles for almost two years. He immediately joined a chorus of other energized officers in I MEF Forward (a chorus led by the Commanding General) to confront and query requirements officials at Quantico, and inform the Pentagon. When confronted with this evidence in communications, Quantico officials stammered. They were caught flat-footed when they learned that an industrious, concerned, and equally determined Lieutenant Colonel in a key stateside billet had assisted Gayl and his fearless Colonel supervisor in Iraq by unearthing the original request that had been buried at MCCDC in 2005, apparently to escape oversight. But I MEF Forward had many other irons in the fire, and a definitive investigation of what had happened would need to await Gayl's return to the Pentagon in 2007.

Overcoming the immediate threat to Marines in Al Anbar was his Commanding General's, and therefore his own, first priority. In this (amongst several other initiatives), Gayl supported his supervisors by helping to accelerate the delivery of many thousands of vehicles above and beyond those which had already been requested. Around Christmas of 2006, he recommended replacing most of the over 4,000 armored HMMWVs belonging to the Marines in Iraq with MRAPs. The HMMWVs would always be available for lower risk missions that absolutely required them, but missions outside safe bases requiring MRAP-protection would be ever-rarer exceptions. Gayl's "objective" goal was that none of I MEF's Marines, Soldiers, Sailors or Airmen would be deprived of MRAP protection where IED attacks threatened. His advice was welcomed by the Commanding General, and constituted the command's urgent request back to the Pentagon and Quantico.

Gayl's determination was fueled by the frustration of his superiors in Iraq. Sharing their concern for the high price that had been paid by his fellow-Marines, he began to communicate his concerns directly to his Pentagon superiors, the Office of the Secretary of Defense (OSD), the Joint Staff, and the offices of some members of Congress via e-mail. While his Pentagon superiors mouthed sympathy for Gayl's revelations, they refused to decisively engage the at-that-time corrupted command responsible for establishing requirements that led to funding and fielding, namely the Marine Corps Combat Development Command (MCCDC). In the politicized Corporate-HQ Marine Corps culture, harmony between general officer principles was highly prized – none would step in the other's lane of responsibility for fear of openly challenging their peer's (or superior's) credibility. Harmony was everything – ending the IED emergency with the necessary confrontational frankness was evidently a distant secondary concern for all – that is, except the Generals fighting the war in Iraq.

The OSD, however, was less timid, and requested that Gayl personally present his concerns to high-ranking appointed officials in the

Pentagon upon his return in the spring of 2007. He agreed, and both his Commanding General and his Colonel supervisor in Iraq committed to accompanying him to the presentation. It could be a breakthrough that opened floodgates of effective support to Marines in Iraq.

Before returning to the U.S. with the rotating command element, Gayl helped to initiate dozens of separate Marine Corps Service and Joint requirements and concepts that led to a wide range of armor and non-armor related weapons and equipment solutions. Many of those capabilities continue to benefit Marines in Afghanistan and elsewhere long after the end of the Iraq War. His commander and supervisors in Iraq were well-pleased with his contributions; however, his Pentagon superiors had become increasingly incensed with Gayl's disclosures, and were awaiting his return to address the general officer disharmony he had instigated.

A COLD PENTAGON RECEPTION

After completing his nearly six-month civilian tour of duty in Al Anbar, in early 2007 Gayl headed home to Virginia and the Pentagon. The atmosphere was chilled. Upon arriving in his old office, it was quickly made clear to him by his supervisors that he was now persona non grata in many support establishment and Pentagon offices where he had previously been welcome. The "drama" he had started while in Iraq continued to reverberate and was "NOT appreciated!"

Undeterred, and with the clarity that the IED emergency in Iraq must be tackled, he made the pending presentation to OSD his top priority. Every day of further delay in delivering life-saving MRAPs was directly measured in unnecessary deaths and injuries of Marines in Iraq. After initially authorizing Gayl to brief OSD, his Pentagon supervisors quickly retreated under intense pressure from corporate headquarters general officer peers who were offended by its revealing contents. The general officer leaders within the support establishment – including one who would become Commandant of the Marine Corps in 2010 - demanded that Gayl be prohibited from presenting, and some called for his punishment due to his "troublemaking."

Gayl remained motivated – he had, after all, been forewarned of this reaction by his generals in Iraq, the leaders he greatly admired for rejecting the niceties of the general officer culture in favor of looking after the Marines in combat. Conversely, back in the Pentagon environment, the other generals, including the then-Commandant of the Marine Corps, who had been duped by clever subordinates at Quantico, found the embarrassment and disharmony intolerable, having an apparently different set of priorities. But the issue was much bigger than what this or that general officer felt offended by. It was clear to Gayl that if military and civilian officials culpable in the MRAP tragedy were not held accountable, similar scenarios would play out in the future, and the Marines in harm's way would again pay the price. After all, the same officials remained in their positions of decision-making responsibility at MCCDC, and the generals who had supervised them continued to get promoted, one eventually to the level of a national figure in the form of a Unified Combatant Commander. The dangers of corrupted processes at Quantico therefore remained, and the wars in Iraq and Afghanistan were far from over.

GOING PUBLIC

Instead of welcoming and acting on his disclosures, his beloved USMC responded with a disclosure prohibition and a written rebuke. When Gayl realized that he wasn't going to get the help he needed from his superiors in the Corps, who preferred to cover up the intentional delay, he provided a paper copy of his presentation to OSD. It was quickly reproduced and widely distributed. It got highest level visibility in the Pentagon, and Gayl began to sense that positive change might come from it. He felt that his direct and dire communications with OSD while he was still in Iraq in 06-07 had already helped justify the groundwork for positive change even before he returned. This included the Secretary of Defense's establishment of a "MRAP Task Force."

Gayl also decided that, in the name of speed and public visibility, it was critical to "go public" with his discoveries concurrently. This approach fit well with all he had learned and practiced as a Marine with respect to the effectiveness of "combined arms." He contacted the press with his concerns. Congressional inquiries to his Pentagon desk soon followed. A concerned then-Senator Biden, the premier MRAP advocate in the Congress, demanded ground truth on the matter. It was confirmed to him, his colleague Senator Kit Bond (whose son was serving as a Marine in Iraq), and the public by the Brookings Institute that as many as 700 Marines and Soldiers had died in IED attacks which could have been prevented by the MRAPs which had been delayed by bureaucrats at Quantico during 19 months alone. Based on those fatalities, it was estimated by others that during the same period thousands of surviving warfighters had been maimed for life by the ever-more lethal IED blasts. Senator Biden even wrote President Bush out of concern for what Gayl disclosed, while energizing MRAPs generally and their urgent need.

Just as they were in Iraq, officials in Headquarters Marine Corps and at Quantico remained dazed when the media now shed a bright light on their gross and perhaps criminal negligence. MCCDC middle management was scurrying and scrambling, providing often absurd advice to seniors that would soon be disproved by investigators. Generals not directly involved in past MCCDC decisions desperately sought insight into past processes, on MRAP in particular. Refusing to take the blame for decisions they were not responsible for, they pressed their responsible peers who had long been reassigned and promoted to take the media heat in interviews. The combat general who had requested MRAPs in 2005 hurriedly denied that he had requested MRAPs in order to protect his fellow generals and the Corps' reputation. Then, in an extended interview, the support establishment general who oversaw Quantico requirements processes in 2005 made fantastic and equally refutable claims. These included an assertion that the U.S. lacked the industry capacity to produce MRAPs, and a claim that the IED threat in 2005 required nothing beyond the "gold standard" HMMWV, even though the HMMWV had already long been known to be a "death trap" when attacked by IEDs. Their inaccuracies in responding to Congress and the public revealed the desperation of the corporate HQMC.

Reprisals against Gayl followed in rapid succession. A formal counseling was followed by a formal reprimand, and then a proposal for suspension. But he was determined to continue to act as a forcing function until any remaining delays in weapons and equipment delivery were overcome. He continued to communicate with senior officers outside of his chain of command, to visit members of Congress, and to talk to the media in plain sight, in spite of the consequences. In mid 2007, the Project on Government Oversight (POGO), the Government Accountability Project (GAP), and the Office of Special Counsel (OSC) came to Gayl's defense, and effectively stymied the Marine Corps' efforts to dismiss him. He was safe for the time being.

So, in another tactic, Gayl's supervisors grudgingly authorized Gayl to commence an internal investigation, to continue his inquiries begun in Iraq, and to quantify the causes of the tragic acquisition delays. It was clear to Gayl from the start that the offer was an effort at appeasement so that he could focus his energy on a task that they had no intention of eventually making public. His supervisors cynically predicted severe emotional biases in his products that could be used against him, to pigeonhole him as a disgruntled employee whose opinion was, while "appreciated," unqualified and unworthy of serious consideration. Regardless of the pessimistic outlook, Gayl embarked on his new project with intense energy.

And what he found troubled him even more.

Within a few weeks, he had uncovered the "dirty little secret" that lay behind the Marine Corps failure to supply the troops in the field with adequate armor and other equipment. Uncovered is an exaggeration – he had always suspected it, but now he had evidence to quantify it.

Gayl says the name of that secret is a familiar one: money. One could add reputations, but in the world of the Corporate Marine Corps and its support establishment, money and reputations are indistinguishable – synonymous – one and the same. Money was and remains the dirty secret.

"It was all about money," he says today. "Those Marines in 2005-2007 died as mid- and senior level bureaucrats and some senior officers connived to protect their programs and reputations at all costs. For example, burying the 2005 request for MRAPs was easy – they owned the process. MRAPs would have (and eventually did) cost big money, and that money would have to come from Quantico's favored, established programs on short notice in response to urgent requests. In 2005, at a minimum, those pet vehicle projects included armored HMMWV, Expeditionary Fighting Vehicle (EFV), and the already-programmed Joint Light Tactical Vehicle (JLTV), all of which were irrelevant to the protection of Marines in Iraq."

The most notable objectors to Gayl's disclosures were actually in the defense industry, where MRAP had no major U.S. defense industry champions, and was therefore a competitive threat for resources that would otherwise be spent on armored HMMWVs. Since that time many of the senior officers who reprised against him have retired, and, as predicted, passed through the revolving door into the ranks of U.S. defense industry management. Connections between their active duty activities and future civilian industry employment may be un-provable, but the coincidences are compelling.

For Gayl – who along with the rest of the American public had watched the tragedy of IED carnage progress over months and years – the betrayal was "incomprehensible, the very contradiction of the Marine foundational assumption of every Marine's loyalty to fellow Marines.

"As I dug deeper into the culture and operational procedures at Quantico generally and MCCDC specifically," he remembers, "I discovered that there were long-standing – and very comfortable – relationships between the officers who ran this 'support establishment side' of the Marine Corps and the contractors from whom they purchased supplies and equipment for the troops out in the field. For the officers and the contractors alike, it had long been a 'win-win arrangement,' a familiar pattern throughout the proverbial, but very real, phenomenon of the Military Industrial Complex that infects all U.S. military Services, and those of most other industrialized nations.

"At Quantico, many officers were terminal at the time of their acquisition-related assignments. Only a select few would go on to become general officers. Knowing this, some were planning deliberate transitions to second careers as contractors or civil servants using their active duty support establishment reputations as springboards. If, during their last tours, they had been unable to successfully protect, politically defend, and fiscally grow in scope the requirements, concepts and programs they had been handed, their post-Marine Corps prospects might be dim indeed."

Gayl knew many of these Marines and knew them to be overwhelmingly conscientious advocates of their fellow Marines in harm's way. He believed that they would call a spade a spade and sacrifice/kill a bad program that was not in the best interests of warfighters. He knew them to be above selfish shenanigans, wanting only the best for their comrades – they were Marines at every level.

"One disadvantage of being assigned to requirements, concepts, and procurement-related acquisition positions is that Marines or civilians have little choice over which projects and programs they are given to manage. If each had a choice of selecting only the weapons and equipment solutions guaranteed to help Marines in war, they would certainly do so. But that's not how it works. You are given the project, program or solution that you are assigned, and you make it succeed even when common sense tells you there may be something better. Endless studies have looked at the conflicted psychology that plagues officers, bureaucrats and program managers in the schizophrenic world of military acquisition, but to little avail."

However, there were a few at Quantico who were cleverer, who appeared at ease with these conflicts. For them the combat value of the programs was less relevant, even if they were not in the best interests of Marine warfighters. For example, they knew that they could knight the armored HMMWV as the "gold standard" of protection and bury the MRAP need without resistance. They were "experts," after all. They would also not be held accountable for how weapons and equipment performed in the field over the short term. Time cures everything as memories are short and attribution becomes difficult. However, they would pay dearly in reputation and upward mobility for losing their program resources to upstart "operator bright ideas", like MRAPs. Clever officials are usually the most successful, and predictably they came to fill key positions in Quantico's middle management. As a consequence, Gayl soon realized that contractor influence, direct and indirect, was larger than warfighter influence on support establishment behavior.

The bottom line as it pertained to MRAPs: A major armored vehicle defense contractor had been supplying the Marines with inadequately armored HMMWVs for years prior to the explosion of IED violence that overtook the U.S. occupation of Iraq beginning in 2003. Instead of immediately replacing them with tailor-made commercial MRAPs that Marines in Al Anbar were urgently requesting, the Quantico support establishment buried the request and insisted on HMMWV add-on and factory armor that likewise failed to protect the Marines. And the assured continued delivery of those vulnerable vehicles was governed by long-term relationships between the officer and civilian acquisition officials throughout the DoD, and most significantly the U.S. defense industry, where many eventually land.

The interconnectedness of the military and defense industry is repeatedly confirmed today throughout the DoD. For example, a recently retired four-star Commandant of the Marine Corps was subsequently hired to serve on the board of directors of a major defense contractor. While such post-military employment of a powerfully symbolic figure like the Marine Corps Commandant is in no way prohibited, for some it violates Marine sensibilities regarding propriety at a deeper level. At lower rank levels, the practice is even more widespread and routine.

"It was all about money, nothing but money," Gayl restates again. "The need for MRAPs was known, the consequences of not providing them were predicted, and those consequences were eventually evident. That's why I still believe MRAP was a criminal matter that should have been prosecuted in a court of law. Unfortunately, that was and is not to be. The nation's memory will be short, and the culpable officers and civilians will probably survive unscathed. A class action lawsuit by the survivors of Marines and Soldiers who became victims of IEDs while riding in HMMWVs might be a good alternative. One way or another, this conduct can't be allowed to be repeated in the future. It was a grotesque betrayal."

Utterly disillusioned by the ugly reality that he'd uncovered, Gayl did his best to alert his Marine Corps superiors at the Pentagon through his project. Instead of thanking him for his investigative case studies and referring them to Department of Defense investigators, they sat on the drafts. Gayl predicted that this would happen, and knew that another forcing function might be required. In anticipation, he finished his drafts and signed and submitted them as final. This would force their consideration immediately. By chance, in the spring of 2008, the office of Senator Biden asked for Gayl to provide an update and copies of his now completed unclassified case studies. Those studies quickly found their way to the press. This action forced the Marines to request a formal Inspector general audit when several Senators threatened unilateral Congressional action. The Marine Corps immediately made an effort to disown the studies that they had directed Gayl to conduct, and belittled his findings. Reinforcing Congressional testimony by senior generals quickly followed.

But the futility of attempting to revise the MRAP history was made painfully evident to the Commandant of the Marine Corps during his sworn testimony before the Senate Armed Services Committee (SASC) in early 2008. Following some fact-checking, in a letter that was quickly made public, the late Senator Edward Kennedy – a SASC member – accused the Commandant of misleading Congress. In his letter, Senator Kennedy accused the Commandant of "mischaracterization" of the request for MRAPs and "inaccurate testimony" regarding the Marine Corps' efforts to improve its processes. Gayl is the first to admit that senior officers, especially generals, all want the best for their Marines. But they are "generalists," and absolutely depend on honest subordinates to prepare them properly with details.

MCCDC bureaucrats were especially lacking in this regard on the topic of MRAP. No Marine general, least of all the Commandant, likes to be embarrassed, much less to be called a liar by a U.S. Senator. This is especially true when the public comes to perceive that the generals might have on their hands the blood of their own Marines. While fixing MCCDC's problems was important for the generals, their first priority was to permanently silence the embarrassing and troublemaking messenger, Franz Gayl.

The backlash on Gayl was immediate, some overt, but mostly covert. "First they threatened again to fire me from my civilian job," he remembers. "They let me know that if I didn't shut up, I wouldn't be working at the Pentagon much longer. A new round of reprisals accompanied the threat, including two consecutive years of rock-bottom personnel appraisals that placed me in the bottom three percent of civilian employees. I simply considered it all part of the price of doing my duty. But there were more insidious actions that they launched in the background. Unbeknownst to me, soon after my case study disclosures in early 2008, the Commanding General at MCCDC at that time – who would become the Commandant of the Marine Corps in 2010 – apparently initiated a security-related investigation that recruited the Naval Criminal Investigative Service (NCIS). The fallout from that act of reprisal would not be known to me or affect me until two years later, but when it came about those effects would be devastating."

Gayl's case studies received significant media attention, and led directly to the initiation of a Department of Defense Inspector General audit of the MRAP debacle. One day, in the spring of 2009, Gayl received a letter from Congressman Edolphus Towns, then Chairman of the House Committee on Oversight and Government Reform. Gayl was invited to testify before Congress on his experiences as a whistleblower in support of hearings related to the pending Whistleblower Protection Enhancement Act (WPEA).

After informing his supervisors and requesting a day of leave to testify, Gayl prepared and submitted his written statement.

TESTIFYING BEFORE CONGRESS

On the day of the hearing, he told the committee: "In Iraq I witnessed the tangible costs in lives lost and serious injuries incurred due to the apparent gross mismanagement of requirements at the Marine Corps Combat Development Command (MCCDC) at Quantico.

"The lack of needed equipment that had been requested and de-layed or denied could be directly tied to preventable casualties. The most tragic delays concerned the Mine Resistant Ambush Protected (MRAP) vehicle, the Ground-Based Observation and Surveillance System (G-BOSS), Tier 2 Unmanned Aerial Vehicles, and a number of non-lethal laser and other directed energy devices needed to mitigate civil and checkpoint confrontations, so that it would not be necessary to inadvertently shoot innocent civilians. Despite unambiguous and continuous feedback from the deployed Marines MCCDC at Quantico, the Marine Corps turned a blind eye to requests for urgently needed equipment whenever those requests conflicted with parochial con-cepts or acquisition priorities in a competition for resources."

After pointing out that "as a civil servant, I enjoyed an unblemished record until 2007, when I blew the whistle on a procurement break-down caused by Marine Corps institutions at Quantico, Virginia," Gayl went on to tell the congressional committee that the Marine command-ers had known for some time that their poorly armored vehicles were extremely vulnerable to IEDs:

"Since the mid-1990s, the Marine Corps has known that up-armored High Mobility Multi-Purpose Wheeled Vehicles (HMMWVs) are 'death traps' in their vulnerability to mines because of the HMMWV's flat bottom, low weight, low ground clearance, and aluminum body. The Marine Corps since the mid-1990s has also been aware of the commer-cial availability of fourth-generation mine-resistant vehicle (MRAP) designs and products. MRAP-type vehicles have a V-shaped hull, and protect against the fragmentation, blast overpressure, and acceleration kill mechanisms of mines and improvised explosive devices (IEDs).

"MRAPs provide the best currently available protection against IEDs, as a Marine is four to five times less likely to be killed or injured in an MRAP-type vehicle than in an up-armored HMMWV." – *[Author's note: today we know from the Pentagon officially that MRAPs were and are in fact thirteen (13) times more survivable than armored HMMWVs.]*

Gayl continued in his 2009 testimony: "Yet evidence shows that combat developers knowingly delayed responding to an urgent request for 1,169 MRAPs from Marines in Iraq for a period of what effectively amounted to 19 months.

"As a consequence, hundreds of Marines died and thousands of Marines were permanently maimed in combat unnecessarily."

To say that Gayl was upset by the needless and evidently knowing delays imposed by stateside officials is to understate his reaction by about 1000 percent. "I still shake my head in disbelief," says Gayl, even now, following his partial vindication in a whistleblower case that made front pages all across the country. "These civilian bureaucrats who had misled senior Generals into lying to the press and before Congress had once served as Marines themselves. The United States Marine Corps is my entire life – is my family. I joined at age 17, and the rewards of retirement do not include shedding the Marine character. It was and is supposed to be their family as well. But what they did violated everything we had been taught as Marines – they betrayed their own, and their surviving families as well.

"The idea that the Corporate USMC would allow its own combat soldiers to be killed or injured . . . when those tragic incidents could have been prevented by getting the MRAPs to Iraq when they were needed most – well, that just made me crazy. As far as I was concerned, I had no choice. Once I saw what was going on, back in 2006 and 2007, I *had* to blow the whistle!"

Like so many whistleblowers in recent years, Gayl paid an agonizingly high price for standing up to power and telling the truth about waste, fraud and abuse in the federal government. Describing his long and arduous journey, battling his stonewalling Marine Corps chain of command and disclosing Marine Corps failures to the Pentagon and others, he told the congressional committee in 2009: "The reprisals from my supervisors began in March of 2007, immediately following my return from Iraq.

"It was clear that my chain of command was trying to silence me by punishing me each time I exercised my rights – rights protected by the Whistleblower Protection Act (WPA) and the First Amendment – to disclose the deadly consequences of the Marine Corps procurement process."

Gayl anticipated an immediate reprisal for his 2009 testimony, but his displeased supervisors were both clever and patient. They did recognize the WPA as an impediment to any direct retribution. But they were unconcerned. They had already set in motion over a year beforehand a more insidious plan that, if executed properly by his supervisors in collaboration with NCIS, might disgrace Gayl professionally and force him out of federal government. So he survived another year, but only on borrowed time. During that year he was issued performance improvement programs (PIPs), denied bonuses, received a new position description that proposed to demote and strip him of his science and technology duties, and he continued to get substandard evaluations. But those were not the Corporate Marine Corps' main efforts — only economy of force distractions. The decisive shoe would only drop later, in the fall of 2010.

CLEARANCE SUSPENSION AND ADMINISTRATIVE LEAVE

In spite of his congressional testimony and the visibility of his public disclosures, the nightmare for Gayl continued. On an ordinary workday in the fall of 2010, the nightmare proceeded innocently enough. On that morning, Franz Gayl looked up from his desk to discover that he had an unexpected visit from his supervisor in the top-secret Sensitive Compartmented Information Facility (SCIF) office at the Pentagon where he worked. He was not smiling.

The Colonel approached Gayl's work station cubicle and stated: "Mr. Gayl, I'd like you to come with me, please."

Gayl came quickly to his feet, stating: "Okay, no problem." He was doing his best to maintain a cheerful demeanor. "But can you tell me what this is all about?"

"No, I can't – just follow me."

Gayl did as instructed. After a short trek he found himself standing outside his general's office. Inside, officials sat around a table that was clearly prepared for his arrival. He was invited in by the general.

Once seated, he found himself confronting a civilian human resources staffer, his supervisor, the general's civilian deputy, and the general. Gayl now knew that a renewed reprisal was forthcoming. The bureaucrats in particular exhibited eager compliance. These prior Marines were well aware of Gayl's public disclosures over the years and the validity of many of his assertions. But they had all chosen a different path. It can be convincingly argued that helping the uniformed general officer supervisors to get rid of a troublemaker could only improve their own status. Getting along is a key to careerism anywhere, not just in the Pentagon – and the amorality of kowtowing is generally dismissed as irrelevant.

The general began: "Mr. Gayl, before we proceed, I would like you to read this letter and confirm that you understand its contents."

Gayl took the official-looking missive from the general and quickly scanned its contents. He felt a bit disoriented when he read the heading at the top of the very first page: *Suspension of Access to Classified Information*. He continued to read.

With growing incredulity, he read that he was being accused of abusing his access to classified systems and materials on numerous occasions.

"Credible information exists," the sternly written document pointed out, "which raises serious questions as to your ability or intent to protect classified information."

After pointing out that the NCIS had been secretly scrutinizing Gayl's work habits for over two years, the sinister message went on to announce that, ". . . based on the forensic analysis contained within the [NCIS] report, it appears that on multiple occasions you used an unauthorized USB [Universal Serial Bus] media flash device [an external, detachable tool for storing digital information] within the Sensitive Compartmented Information Facility [SCIF] in violation of SCIF security requirements.

"The culmination of the above demonstrates a disregard for regulations, a pattern of poor judgment, and intentional misconduct."

Gayl gave the letter back to the general and confirmed that he understood it. The general asked him if he had any questions, and, if not, to acknowledge receipt of the letter with his signature. Gayl, who had learned the futility of rebutting these reprising personnel actions in the past, did not have any, and compliantly signed.

Although the letter from Marine HQ did not charge Gayl with intentionally leaking – or even inadvertently exposing – any sensitive information, its intent was crystal clear. And during the unpleasant hour or so that followed, that intent was fully realized. As a life-long dedicated Marine, he was now informed of his administrative rights, dismissed by his general, escorted before various waiting security officials, and summarily stripped of all his security clearances. At each stop, he was "read out" of various accesses and programs. A few officials appeared smug and satisfied, as this ritualistic event was clearly well planned and coordinated, and intended to be a walk of shame.

Gayl had suspected all along that this day might come. With civil servants, one cannot simply fire them for disgracing an organization with embarrassing disclosures. The media had also ensured that public and congressional interest in the issues he had raised would not permit headquarters shenanigans to silence this particular messenger, and OSC was watchful in the background. Indeed, the Marines needed something much stronger as justification, something that could evade transparent oversight.

Fortunately for the Corporate Marine Corps, Gayl was extraordinarily vulnerable. Because of his space and Information Operations-related job functions, Gayl possessed high security clearances and worked in an extremely sensitive workspace. He had knowledge of various activities which demanded strictest secrecy and accountability. If he could be deemed untrustworthy, he could be stripped of his accesses. Without his accesses, he could not enter his workspace or do his job. His appeal avenues would be quite limited, and most importantly beyond public view and scrutiny.

The Marines would have no problem firing him under such circumstances; in fact, they might even be able to convince him to resign in disgrace, washing their hands. Today it was clear to him that the dreaded day had finally arrived.

In spite of the seeming inevitability of this day, at another level Gayl could hardly believe what was happening. He'd spent almost a decade working in these top-secret environs. In fact, he was one of the most experienced civilian defense analysts and advisors in the entire Department of Plans, Policies and Operations. Gayl had spent literally thousands of hours entrusted with Top Secret Sensitive Compartmented Information (TS/SCI) and other unique clearances and materials. Prior to his return from Iraq in early 2007, his performance reviews had all been routinely outstanding – his trustworthiness, judgment, and reliability had never been questioned. In fact, in his evaluation of Gayl, his Commanding General in Iraq had recommended that Gayl be considered for promotion into the Senior Executive Service. And, considering his years of approved and unsupervised access, how could anyone accuse him of not being able to protect classified information?

Nevertheless, by eleven in the morning Gayl found himself placed on "paid administrative leave." His supervisor, who had escorted him throughout the morning out-processing, directed the official Pentagon vehicle driver to drop him off at the nearest off-site public bus stop. There his supervisor presented him with the administrative leave suspension letter. His last act was to confiscate Gayl's Pentagon badge and ask Gayl to leave the vehicle and the Pentagon premises.

In the space of two hours, Franz Gayl's decades-long career as a Marine had come to a screeching halt.

"It was all about cutting me down to size and humiliating me," he will tell you quietly, while describing how he rode the public transit back to his home in Northern Virginia that morning. "But of course, they knew and I knew that these were contrived charges motivated by a very different purpose.

"The real lesson they were teaching me, and more importantly the others who watched the spectacle, was what happens to people who expose abuses of power in the corporate Marine Corps. Whether you are military or civilian, you do not embarrass the Marine Corps leadership. The USB flash-drive incident was just a red herring."

As to the Marine Corps' specific accusation, Gayl stated: "Anything is possible, and if I had recalled an offense they accused me of I would have admitted it. Of course they could have asked me at the time of the discovery of the alleged security incident more than two years earlier. That omission itself was very curious. Additional NCIS investigation irregularities and delays raised further suspicions. "I, an *"untrustworthy, unreliable employee possessing poor judgment"* had with complete general officer knowledge retained unsupervised access to some of the nation's most sensitive secrets for over two years after the alleged incident, without being informed that I was suspected of anything." Under any normal circumstance, his supervising generals between 2008 and 2010 could have been charged with gross or even criminal negligence for knowingly jeopardizing U.S. national security through this ill-advised office mischief. But these were anything but normal circumstances – the objective was clear, and Gayl was the target.

"And the certainty of my accusers didn't pass the 'sniff test.' During that entire period any other SCIF colleague, including my enraged supervisor or one of his subordinate sycophants, could have poisoned my computers with a log entry of a flash drive insertion as grounds for asking for an NCIS inspection. There was ample opportunity for such mischief. In our secure office all cleared employees enjoyed unfettered access to each other's work stations during short absences of the responsible, logged-in operators. The command motive for such mischief was intense.

"After my disclosures in 2007, the command climate – starting with the Commandant of the Marine Corps – exerted intense pressure on my supervisors to see that I quit or be terminated. Poisoning my computers, as grounds for asking for an NCIS inspection, would have been consistent with the other irregularities and precedents set by my supervisors to retaliate against me for those disclosures. Interestingly, the Marine and NCIS accusations didn't pass the federal court sniff test either. I learned from an unnamed officer that, during their over two year hush-hush investigation, NCIS approached the U.S. District Court in Alexandria, Virginia, seeking a warrant to raid and search my home. It was denied to them by the court due to a lack of probable cause or sufficient evidence."

The DoD IG, separately unhappy with Gayl for his recent criticism of the timidity of their MRAP and other IG audits, compliantly rubber-stamped both NCIS's conclusions and Gayl's Marine Corps supervisors' removal of his clearances. The outspoken Gayl had clearly become a pariah throughout the DoD.

"While anything is possible, I contend that this accusation was retaliation, pure and simple. The words of my supervisor at the time the NCIS investigation was apparently initiated in early 2008 should have been a clue. While escorting me to the general's office to receive the first of many formal reprisals in 2007 he stated: 'Okay, you went public with your information about the Marine Corps' failure to get MRAPs to Iraq. No procurement system is perfect. But you hung the generals and senior officers out to dry, and now you're going to pay a price for that.'"

As an interesting footnote, the general at MCCDC who oversaw the initiation of the NCIS investigation in 2008 would be promoted to Assistant Commandant, and later Commandant, of the Marine Corps in 2010. As the smallest Service, coincidences are frequent as professional career paths cross regularly. He knew Gayl well, as he had once been Gayl's Pentagon supervisor. In 2002, that same general, as a one-star, had personally presided over the retirement of then-Major Gayl in the center courtyard of the Pentagon to great fanfare. In a long speech, he lauded Gayl for his forthrightness and dedication to the Corps, and even presented him a medal, the second from that general. In fact, afterwards, that same general was responsible for rehiring Gayl as a GS-15-equivalent civilian science and technology advisor, a double promotion to the civilian equivalent of a full bird Colonel. But Gayl's praised, past forthrightness had never criticized the Corps. The general must have confused Gayl's enthusiasm for the Corps with blind subservience, and expected the same in the future. However, beginning in 2006, Franz Gayl had out of necessity crossed swords with the corporate Marine Corps, and in 2010 his 2002 reputation was a distant memory. It was therefore no coincidence that on the very same morning that his old supervisor was confirmed as the new Marine Corps Commandant in a Senate vote, Gayl was marched out of the Pentagon. While such management hypocrisy is part and parcel to civilian corporate behavior, the irony that it infected the Marine Corps leadership still amazed him.

When Gayl committed to the path of correcting the corrupted urgent acquisition process while he was still in Iraq in 2006, he was cautioned by his upright and fearless general officer superiors there that he would encounter a long and demoralizing road ahead when he returned to the Pentagon. So, while unpleasant, the most recent humiliations were expected. Instead of complaining about his present dilemma, he looked to the past for inspiration, especially from his deceased father, whom he cherished and modeled his conduct upon.

INSPIRATION FROM HIS FATHER

When Franz Gayl was a boy growing up in Minnesota, he learned some very powerful lessons about duty and compassion from a father whose own extraordinary life reads like a novel by Tolstoy. A fiercely dedicated youth who grew up in Berlin during the Third Reich, Franz Joseph Ferdinand Gayl had served as a devoted member of both the Hitler Jungvolk (Nazi cub scouts) and a young leader in the Hitler Jugend (Nazi boy scouts). Then one day the outwardly Aryan Gayl came to be informed by his family that his beloved mother had in fact been born Jewish! Fortunately, he came from a connected family, and was protected by his paternal Uncle Bruno, who then served as an influential member of the Nazi Party.

Young Franz was a ferociously proud German. He had aspired to be an officer in the Wehrmacht or the Schutzstaffel (SS). Naturally, he was now barred from the officer ranks because of his biological heritage, and a mere application would have jeopardized his mother, at a minimum. However, Franz Gayl Senior remained determined to serve and fight as a soldier in Hitler's Third Reich. Following wise counsel from his Uncle Bruno, he wound up enlisting in the less-politicized *Luftwaffe* as a paratrooper. He excelled immediately as a machine gunner in the tough-as-nails and soon-to-be legendary military organization. Following a tour as a junior jump instructor, he entered World War II combat at Tobruk in North Africa, and later participated in the

Battle of El Alamein. He was subsequently captured by the British and then turned over to the Americans, only to spend the last two years of the war in U.S. POW camps located in Texas and Maryland.

Like so many other Germans, Franz Senior was disillusioned by the war, not just by the defeat but even more so by its industrial-scale cruelty. Following repatriation, he returned to Berlin with the determined intent to build a more compassionate Germany and world. Amazingly enough, the passionate German soldier had been so enthralled by America that he vowed to someday immigrate to the United States . . . which is precisely what he did a few years later, studying at the University of Chicago, earning an architectural degree, and marrying Franz Gayl Junior's – also part-Jewish – American mother in Minnesota.

Deeply influenced by his father's creative and intense *Fallschirmjäger* spirit and iron commitment to duty, Franz Gayl Junior was also deeply affected by his father's depression and parents' eventual divorce. As a high school student, he began "acting out" by engaging in rebellious, anti-social and destructive behavior. All too soon, he found himself "getting into a whole lot of trouble that nearly derailed any military aspirations I might have had, even before a career got started."

But he was very lucky. "I was a bad actor," he recalls, "a really knuckleheaded kid. I think the term 'juvenile delinquent' is actually too mild to describe the kind of attitude I had back then. But I got a huge break, because in those days, the Marine Corps and the Army still routinely took 'problem kids' into their ranks. Those were the 'old days,' the post-Vietnam world of 1974 – really, I'm sure you couldn't even get *into* the Marine Corps these days with the kind of baggage I was carrying, much less the behavior that I was exhibiting as a soon-to-be 17-year-old high school drop-out.

"But the Marines were exactly what I needed. They took a chance on me, and quickly knocked some sense and humility into me. They taught me what real strength is – the strength that comes from self-discipline – and they taught me how to act like a gentleman. They taught me there were things greater than my own self-interests.

"I owe much of this to the Marines, but I owe even more to my father. In addition to his compassion and idealism he had an unbreakable will of steel – he seemed immune to physical pain and hardship, and was even less impressed by the weak human trend towards conformity in order to avoid unpleasantries. He lived from the heart and placed others first. In fact, I volunteered to attend Army Airborne and Ranger Schools specifically as a salute to my father's *Fallschirmjager* heritage. He held the Marine Corps in highest esteem and expected me to live up to its values. I knew I had often fallen short, but looking back at my father as inspiration during my current exile, I refused to fail to see the current challenge through, no matter the personal cost.

"My father would have expected it, and he would have expected me to be particularly resilient in the face of the corporate leadership weakness and hypocrisy that I witnessed. I knew that I would always fall short of my father's willpower, but I had always committed to at least modeling him.

"And I also had and have an equally inspiring living role model in my stepfather Arthur Pejsa, himself a WWII warrior who had flown 400 combat hours over Japan as a pilot in command of a B-29. Today, as one of the few remaining B-29 pilots from that intense air war, he always thanks the Marines for their sacrifices on Iwo Jima where he made three emergency landings of combat-damaged aircraft following Japan bombing missions that would not otherwise have made it back to Tinian. With such another man of steel character and courage to look up to, I indeed had much to live up to, so I hung in there."

THE DREADED PSYCH EVAL, AND AN URGENT MEETING

When Franz Gayl's attorney called me in January of 2011, I immediately suggested that we meet at a neutral location where I could interview Franz and then try to help him plan his strategy for the brutal struggle that undoubtedly lay ahead. The attorney liked that plan. But then he went on to point out that his client had recently been ordered to submit to a "psychiatric fitness for duty" exam by a psychologist at the Bethesda Naval Hospital, located in a Maryland suburb of Washington, D.C.

As soon as I heard about the order, my radar went on "red alert".

"I hope you didn't advise him to take that exam," I told the attorney.

"Well, I'm not sure he has a choice," he replied.

"He does. Please tell Franz that I strongly urge him *not* to take the exam," I pleaded with the lawyer. "Those exams are standard operating procedure for any bureaucrat who wants to get rid of an employee. Once they declare that you're mentally incompetent – and that's the usual outcome of the exam – the ball game is over. He'll be forced out of his job, and it will be virtually impossible for him to get it back."

"Thanks for the warning, Don."

"No problem," I said. "And another thing – even if Franz *does* decide to take the exam, at some point down the road, he shouldn't do so without an advance look at their file on him. It's vitally important to know what's coming during that exam, and the examinee has a due-process right to review his or her personnel file before taking it."

Once again, the attorney thanked me . . . and then promised to convey all of this to Franz, along with my suggestion that we powwow as soon as possible.

Franz agreed, and we met near my office in Ellicott City, Maryland, a northern suburban of Washington, D.C. I found him to be a man of high intelligence who had somehow kept his sense of humor – in spite of having endured the kind of endless, punishing adversity that would have floored most whistleblowers. Was it his tough-as-nails Marine Corps training that had protected him from sinking into a crippling depression . . . like so many of the truth-tellers I've counseled over the past three decades?

Whatever the cause, Gayl's upbeat demeanor and hopeful outlook were positive indicators that suggested he wouldn't crack under the pressure of doing battle with the U.S. Pentagon. And that battle was about to begin in earnest.

Gayl seemed feisty and unafraid. But when he handed me the "Forced Fitness for Duty Psychiatric Examination" directive he'd received from the Marine Corps headquarters, I must admit that I felt a surge of alarm. Written in bloodless bureaucratese, the bland document contained an outrageous demand: the Marines wanted Gayl to submit to the exam ASAP – and they had no intention of allowing him to look at the psychological file they had on him.

After studying their request for several minutes, I gave him a long, hard look.

"I hope you haven't decided to go and take this exam," I said.

He stared at me. "I don't think I have a choice," he said with a frown. "I've been told that if I don't agree to meet their psychologist and submit to their exam, they'll fire me for insubordination. I'm on 'administrative leave' right now, of course, but at least I'm still being paid. If they fire me, I'll have no income. I think I need to bite the bullet and take this exam, Don."

I shook my head. "Not true," I argued. "As a matter of fact, their fitness for duty exam is not only unethical, it's arguably *illegal*. I'll tell you what: why don't you at least let me go to the exam *with* you? I've located some psychiatric evidence by a world-class expert that will show that psychologist exactly why participating in this 'forced exam' could involve him in medical malpractice.

"If I can talk with him before you do, we may be able to prevent him from giving the Pentagon the tool they need in order to fire you."

He looked at me carefully. "What tool is that?"

"It's simple," I told him. "If they can get the shrink to say you're 'mentally incompetent' to perform your duties, they'll be authorized under federal law to give you the boot. And believe me, they won't hesitate to do just that."

Franz didn't hesitate. "Okay," he said. "I hear you loud and clear. The exam is set for next Wednesday morning at ten, at the Bethesda Naval Hospital. I'll meet you in the front lobby a few minutes before, all right?"

A MEETING AT BETHESDA

The psychologist turned out to be a soft-spoken Navy Captain with a surprisingly relaxed and easygoing approach to his job. Although he refused to let me sit in on the exam with Franz Gayl, he did agree to talk with me before the exam began. And instead of acting angry and defensive, he seemed friendly and cordial as he led me into his office and pointed me toward a chair.

"How can I help you, Dr. Soeken?"

I thanked him for his courtesy and quickly explained that the psychiatric fitness for duty exam he'd been ordered to perform was a bad idea. Then I pointed out that no less an authority than the American Psychiatric Association (APA) had previously determined that such forced exams were inherently unfair to the examinee . . . and that performing them could amount to malpractice on the part of the examining psychologist or psychiatrist.

My host listened carefully, but seemed skeptical. I was prepared for that, however – and I quickly explained to him that a few years earlier I had served as a consultant to the APA's Committee on Abuse of Psychiatry. While advising the Committee, I'd worked on several occasions with an eminent practicing psychiatrist, Richard S. Epstein, M.D., an acknowledged national authority on the ethical problems that surrounded these compulsory exams.

For the record I had come prepared, having read an authoritative summary (entitled **Validity of Forced Psychiatric Fitness for Duty Examinations**) of Dr. Epstein's finding that these forced psychiatric tools were inherently unfair to those who were compelled to take them – and that they amounted to little more than an arbitrary weapon which could be used by managers to get rid of employees they didn't like, for any reason whatsoever. Dr. Epstein's description of the flawed exams didn't mince words. Although I did not read the exact words of his testimony, I paraphrased his statements in a short speech on the subject of forced fitness for duty exams.

"Employer-mandated psychiatric fitness for duty examinations are generally highly unreliable," he wrote at the beginning of his well-known article on abuses of psychiatry, "and they possess low scientific validity for a number of reasons."

A moment later, Dr. Epstein explained exactly why these exams (which are strictly prohibited among employees of the legislative and executive branches of government, except in cases involving a government security clearance) are so flawed, and why they have the potential to grievously injure the subjects:

"1. They are too easily misused by employers who may wish to rid themselves of an employee, particularly when the employee is functioning satisfactorily on the job and is not exhibiting any abnormal behavior on the job.

2. By using the highly intrusive mechanism of a psychiatric examination, history, and diagnosis, which examines a person's thoughts, feelings and fantasies (not just their actual behavior), almost any examinee can be stigmatized as potentially unsafe or unstable, even though their overt functioning and demeanor on the job is exemplary. In the former Soviet Union, forced psychiatric examination and treatment were misused in this manner to punish and control dissidents who were critical of the regime, but had not broken any of its laws.

3. The essential point is that a forced psychiatric exam should not be used as a measure of pathology in the absence of overt behavior that is significantly dangerous, pathological or illegal.

4. Psychiatric evaluations often contain speculative conclusions based on highly subjective observations."

After I had paraphrased from Dr. Epstein's powerfully argued study, I looked the military psychologist in the eye. "I can't tell you not to perform this exam," I told him. "Proceed, but the potential for these exams [to involve] *malpractice* is quite real in these situations where the subject is compelled to submit to the exam."

The psychologist thanked me and proceeded to the exam.

Although privacy strictures prohibit me from disclosing the specific contents of Franz Gayl's exchange with his Navy Doctor, his recollections of the exam conclusion as we departed the Bethesda Naval Hospital speak volumes about what had just taken place.

Gayl told me: "After the interview was complete, the Doctor asked me if I think that I am crazy. I responded that no, I do not think that I am crazy, but then quickly added that such a response must be expected from any person who *is* truly crazy. He then responded that if I was crazy he would know by now, and I am indeed *not* crazy." For Gayl, that cordial goodbye was a crucially important moment.

EPILOGUE

Less than a year later, he would win a huge victory in his ongoing whistleblower case. Gayl's faithful supporters at POGO and GAP had energized the public to prompt Defense Department intervention. Also, after considering all of the evidence presented by various agencies, including Gayl's Marine Corps supervising generals, the Department of the Navy favorably adjudicated and returned to Gayl the top secret clearance that his Generals had suspended. Simultaneously, the Merit Service Protection Board (MSPB), after being petitioned by OSC, had ordered the Marine Corps to end his more than one year administrative leave and restore his meaningful Pentagon job duties to him. The battles are far from over at the detailed level, but the tables have certainly turned.

Unlike most whistleblowers, Franz Gayl had beaten the odds. Described throughout the national news media as a "hero" who'd risked his career in order to tell the truth about abuses, he was now being praised at the highest levels of the federal government, including by the Vice President of the United States.

However, Gayl refused to gloat over his victory.

"I wasn't happy to see the Marine Corps get a black eye over this case, and frankly I never aspired to being remembered as a whistleblower," he said quietly during our last meeting in late 2011. "I've spent my life serving this proud organization that I greatly revere, doing my small part to keep it relevant as a unique and effective fighting force.

"But my first loyalty is to the young Marines themselves who are willing to put their lives at risk in order to protect us. I was once one of them, and they could just as well be my kids today. They deserve better than just the hollow ceremonial pomp and circumstance of the Corporate Marine Corps. They need tangible action – the support establishment needs to do its job, even if that means sacrificing self-interest. And of course I would do it all again. I wouldn't be much of a Marine if I didn't."

Gayl concludes: "Semper Fidelis needs to be lived and not just mouthed. There was nothing exceptional about what I did in simply keeping faith with my fellow Marines. It's ingrained in our tradition: a Marine does what needs to be done for the sake of fellow Marines who are in harm's way."

SIX

INSIDE THE "ENDLESSLY CORRUPT" WORLD

OF W. VA. COAL MINING

I n 1989 the former US Justice Department Attorney Vincent Laubach
went to work at the US Department of the Interior as Coordinator of
Collection. And that's when he discovered more than a million dollars'
worth of long-overdue fines, penalties, and fees that hadn't been collected during the Carter administration.

Eventually, Laubach was assigned to collect more than $200 mil-
lion in long-overdue strip-mining fines that had been levied against
polluting coal companies during the Ronald Reagan years. At first he
thought it would be "a pretty simple task" to round up the missing monies and turn them over to the U.S. Treasury Department.

He was wrong.

After less than one year of working hard to correct the past negligence – during which he worked endless 12-hour days in a doomed
effort to collect the dollars the coal operators owed Uncle Sam – the
frustrated Laubach realized that it was hopeless.

Protected by the Reagan White House, which was doing its best to
make sure the Justice Department didn't interrupt "business as usual"
in the coalfields of Appalachia, the polluting coal operators had no intention of paying the fines.

Suddenly, Vince Laubach was facing a brutally difficult decision. Should he "go public" with his inside information about how one of America's largest energy industries was routinely cheating U.S. taxpayers out of millions of dollars each year?

Laubach, a faithful Roman Catholic who'd once been a Latin-spouting altar boy during a childhood in which he often dreamed of becoming a priest, knew he didn't have a choice. He blew the whistle on the U.S. Department of the Interior's failure to collect the monies that were due Uncle Sam – and he paid a huge price for his insistence on integrity and honesty.

Because Laubach kept demanding that the U.S. Government collect the nearly $200 million the coal companies owed the U.S. Treasury for creating (and then mostly abandoning) more than 6,000 strip mines throughout the region, the feds tried to take his job in the early 1980s. As I later pointed out in Mother Jones magazine, while describing the outrageous decision to fire Laubach in an article that was headlined River of Trouble:

"Although federal agency officials insist that the actual losses to the U.S. Treasury [from failure to collect the fines] amounted to between $100 million and $200 million between 1978 and 1990, a nine-month investigation into the mess at Interior shows the actual figure to be at least a half-billion dollars. Similar lenience toward the coal industry by state regulators (mainly in Kentucky and West Virginia) over the same period added at least another $500 million to the delinquent fines . . . for a total taxpayer subsidy of at least $1 billion to the U.S. coal industry during the Carter and Reagan years.

"These disturbing conclusions stem from records revealed in a lawsuit brought against Interior by the Save Our Cumberland Mountains environmental group, and in numerous court orders issued by now re-tired U.S. District Court Judge Barrington D. Parker, who ruled repeatedly that Interior must implement drastic reforms."

After summarizing the pollution horrors that had been visited on Appalachia by the coal companies, the Mother Jones report went on to describe Laubach's valiant whistle-blowing over a period that lasted more than a decade: "Attorney Vince Laubach, a longtime conservative

Republican who during former President Ronald Reagan's first term was hired to coordinate all of Interior's coal-mining collection efforts, says that he made the mistake of actually believing that 'Ronald Reagan was serious when he said that he wanted to eliminate waste and fraud in government.'

"But Laubach adds that when he tried to bill the coal operators for back assessments, the higher-ups at his agency put the clamps on him in a hurry. In December of 1982, according to Laubach, after a futile protest to the inspector general and after going public with his campaign to collect the fines, he was fired."

Years later, looking back on the reprisals he faced because he tried to do his job, Laubach would clench his fists in helpless frustration. "It was all pretty tragic," he would remember. "I was able to identify well over $100 million that should have been collected for taxpayers. But they blocked me at every turn, and the money was lost."

As my Mother Jones article later concluded: "A follow-up report by the House Committee on Government Operations made it clear that Laubach was a hero" [while also noting]: "The Department of the Interior has failed miserably to efficiently and effectively carry out its responsibilities for assessing and collecting civil penalties and for implementing other enforcement provisions of the Surface Mining Control and Reclamation Act.

"Later still, Laubach won both an award from the Coalition to Stop Government Waste and a legal settlement that offered him his job back and $24,000 in damages. 'I do feel vindicated,' he said. 'But the taxpayers haven't been, and they were also hurt.'"

DEATH AT BUFFALO CREEK AND "THE MIRACLE BABY"

For West Virginians and outsiders who have reported on coal mining in this often benighted state, the depressing story of Vince Laubach's doomed struggle to make the industry pay for the pollution caused by strip mining was all too familiar.

Indeed, the continuing catalogue of mining-related tragedies reaches back decades . . . reaches all the way back, in fact, to the dreadful morning of February 26, 1972, when a coal company waste-water dam collapsed at Buffalo Creek (located about 70 miles south of Charleston) and wiped out an entire valley, leaving more than a hundred people dead and several thousand homeless.

The story of what happened at Buffalo Creek that day has become the stuff of legend in recent years – and that legend was captured on the page by my good friend and fellow-reporter Tom Nugent, who covered the disaster in great depth for the Detroit Free Press. As Nugent would later note in a book that explored the social dimensions of the catastrophe – along with the reckless corporate decision-making that contributed heavily to it – the suffering and the loss that took place in southern West Virginia as the result of the killer-flood was nowhere more evident than in the heart-rending story of "The Miracle Baby" of Buffalo Creek.

Only an infant at the time of the disaster, Kerry Lee Albright survived through astonishing luck. His story was captured in compelling detail in Nugent's 1973 book, Death at Buffalo Creek, which told the tale of The Miracle Baby's survival in simple, understated prose. That story actually began about an hour before the dam broke, as Kerry Lee's father – Robert Lee Albright – made his way home after working the late shift in an underground mine, as follows:

While Oldie Blankenship fought for his life at Italy Bottom, forty-two-year-old Robert Lee Albright was struggling frantically to reach his family in Lorado. Albright, a soft-spoken, bespectacled coal miner, had finished his hoot owl shift at Buffalo Mining's No. 8B mine around 7:45 and then, as usual, had climbed aboard a mechanized coal belt for the mile-long ride out of the mine. The trip on the rumbling, electric belt would take about fifteen minutes, and then Albright would jump in his car and head home for breakfast.

After twenty-five years in the coal mines around Buffalo Creek, Albright knew every phase of the mining operation. Beginning as a novice coal loader in 1946, he had worked his way up through the ranks. By 1972, he was making $42.80 a day as a skilled electrician – and the bosses, respecting his obvious expertise, were allowing him to work almost as many hours of overtime as he wanted.

It was a good life, nothing like the terrible years of poverty, which Albright had endured as a child. The son of a lifetime coal miner who raised eleven children on his skimpy wages, Albright knew what it was like to struggle along from day to today, always short of money. The Albright kids had not gone hungry ("Potatoes and beans, that was it!"), but Robert had quit school after the sixth grade mainly because "You didn't have no clothes decent to wear." As he learned the hard lessons of poverty, the young Albright swore that he would do a better job of providing for his own family.

He did. Nowadays, the Albrights – Robert, his wife Sylvia, his seventeen-year-old son Steve, and his newly adopted baby, Kerry Lee – lived in a warm, well-furnished home in upper Lorado, a few dozen yards above the schoolhouse. The family drove two cars, ate steak whenever they wanted it. And in a few months, Robert would be sending his son, a talented saxophone player, off to study music at Fairmont State College.

All in all, Robert Albright considered himself better off than he had ever been. He had suffered some terrible disappointments along the way, of course: the death of his oldest son (killed in Vietnam in 1970) was still a daily source of pain. The boy's death had been almost more than Sylvia could stand. Plunged into a deep depression, she had finally required hospitalization for a time. Lately, though, taking care of the new baby they had adopted to help fill the vacuum, she seemed to be regaining her enthusiasm for life.

There were other problems. After twenty-five years underground, Albright's life in the coal mines was beginning to take its physical toll. Since 1963, he had been drawing disability benefits for the bad case of silicosis, which made his breathing painful and difficult. Only a few weeks ago, the doctors had also determined that Albright had miners' pneumoconiosis – black lung – and had certified him for additional benefits. But he kept on working. He felt that he and Sylvia were "Living for them two boys, they was our whole life," and he had been glad enough to sacrifice his health for them.

Friday night's hoot owl shift had been colder than most, but otherwise routine. Working with his helper, a fellow-miner named Tunis

Sipple, Albright had spent most of the shift repairing a malfunctioning coal loader. Halfway through the shift, he and Sipple had paused, fired up an old welder, which they used to keep themselves warm, and eaten the lunches they carried in their tin pails. After the half-hour break, it was back to work. The wiring problem inside the coal loader was the kind of challenge Albright enjoyed. It was part of the reason he preferred coal mining to other jobs. Whenever he thought about doing some other kind of work, Robert remembered his ill-fated experiment of a dozen years ago, when he had left West Virginia to take a job in a Dunkirk, Indiana, bottle factory. The work was boring, endless ("Seemed like it took your shift forever to go by!"), and after only two months, Albright had repacked his bags and returned to Buffalo Creek. The coalmines might be gloomy and dangerous, but at least they offered a variety of jobs and challenges.

Now the belt rattled through the underground darkness. Albright lay on his back staring at the roof of the mine as was pulled toward the surface. Idly, he wondered if his family would be waiting in Lorado to greet him. Steve and Sylvia had planned to drive up to a band concert at Morris Harvey College in Charleston that morning, but the heavy rain might have meant a last-minute postponement. Robert figured, as he rode the vibrating belt a few yards from Tunis Sipple, that they were probably still at home.

Suddenly, the belt stopped. For a moment, he lay motionless in the dark, half-expecting it to begin turning again. But nothing happened. As Albright and Sipple climbed off the belt and began a half-mile walk back to the portal, they discussed the sudden power shutdown. Robert had never seen it happen before. The failure was irritating, but Albright knew nothing of the problem at the Three Forks dam, and made no connection between the two. Emerging from the mine portal at a few minutes past eight, he jumped into his lightning-yellow Gremlin and began the ten-minute drive out of the mountains and down the hollow toward home.

Entering Buffalo Creek Hollow at Pardee, Albright was stunned at what lay before him. The hollow had become a funnel through which thirty feet of black water went plunging along, taking out every structure in its path. He gripped the steering wheel. One by one, the homes along the road were being flattened. Already, the water had torn the Pardee electrical station out of the ground – hurling sparks and flame high in the air – and sending its giant transformers bouncing down the hollow. Trapped helplessly in his car, Albright prayed that his family had gone to Charleston for the band concert after all. If they were still sitting in the house at Lorado and had received no advance warning, he knew they were doomed. Bolting out of the Gremlin, he began to fight his way along the rugged hillsides above the hollow. It was more than half a mile down to his house at Lorado. Ignoring the pain in his lungs, he battled through the thick, tangled scrub. But his heart sank inside him. Already, he knew he was too late.

The Albrights, as it turned out, had received no warning. Seventeen-year-old Steve was standing in the backyard when the water arrived. He raced back inside the house, and a moment later emerged with his mother, who carried nine-month-old Kerry Lee in her arms. Desperately, the three fought their way through the rising water, almost reaching the hillside, which stood a few dozen yards behind their house. But they had started too late. The water rose to their waists, then to their shoulders. The current began to push them down the hollow.

Neighbors who survived the flood later described a pathetic scene: Sylvia standing almost at the bottom of the slope, swinging the baby back and forth through the air, trying to find the strength to throw him up to the crowd on the hill. Finally, the child dropped out of her arms, and in clear view of the horrified people above all three were swept away.

A few minutes later, reaching his own neighborhood at last, Robert Albright had his worst fears confirmed. Everything was gone. Only the bare foundations remained to show him where his house had been. The main wave had passed through Lorado by now, but the water was still shoulder-deep in most places. Albright plunged in. He would swim his way out to where his house had stood. Somehow, he would save them yet. Fighting his way across the torrent, he soon tired to the danger point.

Floundering, choking on the water and the coal-black sludge, he was close to drowning when some men standing on a nearby bank finally threw him a telephone wire. He pulled himself out of the flood on the rescue line, paused to recover some of his strength, and then began asking neighbors if any of them had seen his family. A few minutes later, his last hopes were dashed: the baby had been found wedged in a culvert, facedown, about 100 yards below the house. Had his family gone to Charleston after all, Robert knew they would have first dropped Kerry Lee off at his sister-in-law's house, out of the danger area.

Moving slow as in a dream, the numbed Albright limped to the nearby hose where they had taken Kerry Lee. The little boy was in bad shape. "He was coal-black all over, he looked just like a tar baby. He had a whole patch of skin tore out of his head, and his leg was cut to pieces. They had been working on him – trying to get all that gob out of his throat."

But then a wonderful thing happened. The baby, who had not made a sound since his rescue, began wailing the moment Robert picked him up. It was a strong cry, and Kerry Lee kept it going. Albright figured the battered child would live – if only he could get him to a hospital in time.

Climbing into a neighbor's four-wheel-drive truck, with the baby wrapped tightly in a blanket, Albright began a four-hour nightmare. The only road out of the hollow was blocked by a rockslide. Albright was forced to sit helplessly in the truck while they cleared the slide, even cutting several trees out of the way. Every once in a while they had to get out and walk while the truck was pushed through the rough spots. "We were stumbling along in all this mud and rock. I thought I was gonna break in two."

Finally, they reached the hospital and the baby was rushed to emergency. For three days, Robert did not once leave the child's side, did not even change out of his grimy work clothes until on the third day friends brought him a fresh set. Kerry Lee pulled through the crisis, and the story of his incredible escape quickly passed among the Buffalo Creek residents, who have referred to him as "The Miracle Baby" ever since.

His young son was out of danger, but the bodies of his wife and oldest son had been found, about 800 yards below the home in Lorado, and five days after the flood Albright would have to go down to the morgue to claim them: "My son was crushed up so bad, I went about four times trying to identify him. His head was just smashed to jelly. He had just a little bit of sideburn left, where you could tell it was him. All the bodies had swelled up so bad, you had to just keep looking and looking. . . ."

Robert Albright had sacrificed much of his health to provide for the family he loved. Now, with the oldest son's death in Vietnam, all the members of that family except for Kerry Lee were gone forever. "It was just like a whole lifetime went with a snap of a finger," Albright says. "I killed myself working up there in those lousy mines – but they only killed me little by little. I tell you, if it wasn't for that child, I wouldn't be alive today."

Albright gave up on coal mining. Content to draw his $398 a month in disability payments, he can be found today in one of the temporary trailer parks along Buffalo Creek. He spends his days fixing the baby's bottle, changing the baby's diapers, and occasionally wondering, after all the years of work, what has happened to him.

The Miracle Baby at Age 40, in 2012

Four decades after he somehow survived the disaster at Buffalo Creek, Kerry Lee Albright took a look back at his incredible life. And he talked at length about how – at the tender age of only six months – he'd undergone a devastatingly traumatic experience that by all rights should have killed him.

"I can't tell you how many times I've heard the story of how they tried to throw me up on the hill," says the Brooklyn 40-year-old today. "My mother, Sylvia, and my older brother, Steve . . . I know they fought desperately to save me.

"But they were exhausted, and the water was too much for them. They threw me as far as they could – and then all three of us were swept away by the roaring water. They died. But somehow, I lived.

"Throughout my entire life, I've been known as 'the miracle baby' – and I've been told that there must be a reason why I lived, when so many others didn't."

It happened on a long-ago Saturday morning, when the 40-foot-high wall of water suddenly released by a coal-waste dam went crashing through Buffalo Creek Hollow. By the time the lethal flash flood subsided that morning, 125 residents of the narrow coal-mining valley were dead. Another 4,000 were left homeless . . . and many were forced to spend the next 5-10 years living in "temporary" trailers that had been provided by the U.S. Department of Housing and Urban Development (HUD).

For thousands of Buffalo Creek Hollow residents, that nightmarish event forever altered the landscape they had once called home. With the main highway torn out of the ground in many places – and with the water, sewer and electrical systems completely destroyed – the survivors faced enormous challenges as they struggled to rebuild. And their problems were only exacerbated by disingenuous government officials, both federal and state, who promised but failed to restore public services and support the ongoing effort to create new housing for the thousands who had been forced from the wreckage of shattered homes.

Suffering from numerous physical and psychological problems triggered by the disasters, more than a third of the valley's 5000 residents left the region forever. But Kerry Lee Albright and his father, Robert – the only survivors of their close-knit family – were among those who stayed on.

In many ways, the story of what happened to the "miracle baby" in the years that followed the 1972 cataclysm mirrors the stories of the other survivors. It is a narrative full of pain and suffering and loss and grief . . . but it's also a story full of courage and resilience and a keenly observant sense of humor.

FACEDOWN IN A CULVERT . . . AND DYING

As you might expect, Kerry Lee Albright remembers nothing about that Saturday morning in 1972 that changed his life forever.

A mere infant at the time, he has no memory of how the raging floodwaters from the just-collapsed dam tore his green-shingled home at Lorado, West Virginia from its foundations and sent it spinning wildly down Buffalo Creek Hollow.

Nor does he recall the heroically desperate – and ultimately successful – efforts that were made to save his life. In order to understand what happened on that dreadful morning 40 years ago, Kerry Lee has had to rely entirely on eyewitness accounts and newspaper descriptions of how his doomed family fought to save him. He knows that his mother and his older brother managed to carry him from the collapsing house at Lorado almost to the side of a nearby hill . . . where a crowd of stunned and horrified onlookers watched the family's agony in stricken silence.

He knows that Sylvia and Steve did their best to fling him up the hillside . . . but that their last-gasp attempt to save him from the torrent fell short. Unable to escape, all three were swept into the merciless current. Within a couple of minutes, the water dragged Kerry – a naked baby whose diaper had been torn away – about 800 yards down the narrow, twisting hollow. There it deposited him, facedown and helpless, in a culvert that flanked the raging torrent.

Kerry Lee knows that several survivors fought their way across the blackened, coal-ridden waters of Buffalo Creek in order to pull him from the current. Struggling desperately, they then used their fingers to dislodge the oily-black coal waste from his throat and start him breathing again.

Ignoring the dead bodies that surrounded them, Kerry's stunned neighbors managed to find a woolen blanket somewhere. They wrapped the infant up carefully, doing their best to keep him warm . . . then gave the precious bundle to the child's father, Robert Albright, a veteran Buffalo Creek coal miner. Albright had been en route to his home in Lorado – after working the overnight (or "hoot owl") shift – when the water struck.

After retrieving the cut and bleeding baby, the desperate father spent the next seven hours fighting his way along washed-out, tree-covered roads, before finally getting the child into care at a hospital emergency room.

At first glance, the battered infant seemed unlikely to survive. His right leg had nearly been cut off at the thigh; it was connected to his body by only a narrow band of lacerated muscle. The baby was covered with deep flesh-cuts and black-and-blue contusions. And he was also suffering from hypothermia, after spending nearly eight hours soaking wet, as the brooding winter skies continued to pelt Buffalo Creek with a mixture of heavy rain and wet snow.

But Kerry Lee didn't die.

Instead, he became "The Miracle Baby" – a figure of local legend in the God-fearing, deeply religious world of southern West Virginia. In this conservative region of Appalachia, dominated by fundamentalist Baptist and Pentecostal churches, fiery preachers proclaim the joys of salvation and the terrors of hell from a thousand pulpits every Sunday morning.

As soon as he could listen and understand what these "men of God" were saying, Kerry Lee was bombarded by endless sermons and homilies in which the "miracle" of his survival was presented as a shining example of the loving kindness of God. He was also told again and again that he was "very special," and that God "must have saved him so he could accomplish some important mission during his time on earth."

It took Kerry Lee more than 30 years to come to terms with the mythology of his own life – with his anxiety-provoking legacy as a "miracle" who had been allowed to survive only because God intervened in his fate at the last moment.

FROM "THE HOLLER" TO VEGAS: A REMARKABLE ODYSSEY

After the debris from the killer flood was finally hauled away, Kerry Lee and his father resumed their lives at Buffalo Creek Hollow. Robert Albright gave up on coal mining and chose to live on his $400-a-month disability payments as a miner who'd contracted a severe case of "black lung" during his years underground.

It was to be a strange and often painful existence. Having lost his wife and his son Steve in the flood, Albright was also grieving for the death of his oldest son Terry – a U.S. Army combat soldier who'd been shot to death by a crazed fellow-trooper in South Vietnam, only a year or so before the disaster at Buffalo Creek.

To this day, Kerry Lee remembers how his father would buy a bottle of whiskey on "anniversary days" – the yearly reminders of Terry's death in the war and the disaster at Buffalo Creek. "Each year he'd arrange for a friend to take care of me," says Kerry Lee, "and then he'd get into the whiskey.

"He'd drink all day long and cry a lot – and then he'd pull out of it and get back to normal. It was just a ritual he insisted on, year after year."

By the time Kerry Lee entered high school, however, the stresses that had been created by Robert's trauma were beginning to impinge on their relationship. As the conflicts between them grew deeper, there were ugly scenes of hostility and struggle.

On one terrible afternoon, during a violent quarrel, Kerry Lee suddenly grabbed his father's heart medication and shook the entire bottle of pills into his mouth at once.

"I shouted at him: 'I want to die!' Kerry Lee recalls today, "and I was shocked by his reaction. His eyes had filled up with tears; all at once he was weeping openly. I spat the pills out and told him I was sorry. That was the worst thing I ever did to my father, and I regret it to this day."

Father and son somehow managed to get through their struggles, however. Meanwhile, Kerry Lee had discovered that he was a talented singer – after a local choir director pointed out that he "had the best voice in the entire Amherstdale Baptist church." Within a few years, the youngster was starring as a singer and dancer in musicals at the local high school and at a nearby community theater. That interest eventually led to a scholarship at Marshall University in Huntington, West Virginia, where Kerry Lee would continue to shine onstage.

During the summer before his senior year at Marshall, he received an offer he couldn't refuse: a chance to sign on with the American Entertainment Corporation as a singer-dancer at one of their permanent shows in a musical theater located at a New York State Park near Buffalo.

It was too good an offer to pass up. Kerry Lee said goodbye to college life . . . and launched what would become a 20-year career as a traveling entertainer. During his two decades as a singer and dancer, he's performed for months at a time at major Las Vegas hotels (including the MGM Grand and the Excalibur), while also serving frequently as a shipboard entertainer for the Carnival Cruise Lines. He's sung and danced his way to a good livelihood . . . and spent many months living in Germany, Mexico, the Caribbean, China and Japan along the way.

Today, at age 40, he lives in a comfortable, ground-floor apartment in the Bushwick section of Brooklyn, New York.

His father died of heart disease back in 2000.

"I've had a very unusual life, that's for sure," says Kerry Lee today. "I grew up almost as the prisoner of my own myth – the idea of me as a 'miracle baby'. Everywhere I would go, people told me that God must've had a plan for me.

"But I have a very different feeling about all of that. I don't think the 'miracle' – if there was one – was about me. I think I survived so that I could comfort my father. So that I could be with him and love him during the bleak years after he lost everyone he cared about.

"He lost everyone except me!"

Déjà Vu All Over Again: Mountaintop Removal Mining in W. VA.

Remember that ancient Chinese saying by the wise old man who'd lived for many years, while watching history unfold all around him?

The more things change, the more they stay the same.

To understand the sage's wisdom fully, all you have to is spend some time in West Virginia – a tattered and economically devastated region of America that has often described as "a colony of New York."

Whether we're talking about valleys that get destroyed by reckless coal operators who don't bother to engineer their projects properly – or about strip-mine fines that never get collected by Uncle Sam – the result is always the same: the region ends up paying a steep price so that outsiders can continue to bleed her dry.

Example: Only a few months before this book was completed, the author published a story in the Huffington Post about the abomination that is "mountaintop removal mining" in West Virginia and the other Appalachian states.

Rather than repeat all the details in "Bombs Away in West Virginia," it might be better to simply run the published story right here – so that readers can see for themselves exactly what we're talking about.

BOMBS AWAY IN WEST VIRGINIA!

Charleston, W. Va. — Ever wondered what would happen if an invading power suddenly attacked the gorgeous, summer-green mountains of Appalachia with massive bombs that together equaled the explosive power of the Hiroshima A-bomb, each and every week?

Amazingly enough, that stark scenario is happening right now in West Virginia, with hardly a whimper of protest from federal government regulators or the state politicians in Charleston.

During the past ten years, in fact, mountaintops all across Appalachia have been blowing up one after another, creating rock-strewn "moonscapes" which now include more square miles than those contained in the entire State of Delaware.

Fact: As of July 1, 2011, these bombers . . . who are now using more than 3 million pounds of explosives each day in West Virginia alone have destroyed more than 500 Appalachian mountaintops.

An environmental catastrophe? You bet it is. Hour by hour and day-by-day, we're witnessing the ongoing destruction of our oldest and perhaps most beautiful mountain chain. And yet most of our politicians – along with most of our news media – seem to be totally unconcerned about the bombing campaign against America.

Maybe that's because the "invading powers" now blasting away at the steep ridgelines of West Virginia, Virginia and Kentucky aren't foreign countries, after all.

They're actually giant U.S. energy companies – hugely powerful industries that long ago became accustomed to dictating energy policy in Washington D.C. and in the state capitals of Appalachia.

How bad is the wholesale destruction now being caused by the ruthless bombing-and-digging technique known as "mountaintop removal mining," all across the once-forested and once-life-abundant region that was America's first frontier?

To answer that question, you only have to look at the most recent data from the state and federal environmental agencies. Those data show how hundreds of surface-mining sites located along the Appalachian range have been attacked with high explosives in recent years . . . so that mega-sized mining machines can go in later and scoop up the coal and then hustle it off to market.

"What they're doing is illegal," says environmental activist Robert Kennedy, Jr., a longtime opponent of Appalachian mountaintop mining as practiced by companies like Massey and Pittston. "If you blew up a mountain in the Berkshires or the Catskills or California or Utah, you would go to jail."

Like Robert Kennedy, the conservation-minded Sierra Club has been fighting this destructive mining technique in recent years, while frequently pointing out that it "has destroyed forests on some 300 square miles of land, disrupted drinking water supplies, flooded communities and destroyed wildlife habitat."

But the mountaintops aren't the only areas, which take a daily beating in Appalachia.

In recent years, the thunderous explosions that are the key to mountaintop removal mining (they can send up to 800 feet of rock flying skyward on a single blast) have buried more than 2,500 miles of Appalachian rivers and streams beneath a tsunami of pulverized stone and earth – much of it tainted with toxic refuse from underground coal mines.

That's right: We're looking at 2,500 miles of once-upon-a-time-pristine creeks and rivers that are now totally choked with mining rubble, all across Appalachia.

And there's more: according to a major study just published in the peer-reviewed Journal of Community Health: The Publication for Health Promotion and Disease Prevention, the cancer rate among people living beside a West Virginia mountaintop removal site in recent years was twice as high as the rate among those living a safe distance away from the site. The bottom line on that disturbing study: at least 60,000 cases of mining-linked, above-the-norm cancer can be expected among the 1.2 million West Virginians who live near these mining sites in West Virginia, within the next few decades.

So where's the outcry?

Why aren't the senators and the congressional reps from places like West Virginia and Kentucky raising holy hell in the echoing hallways of the Senate and the House?

The answer isn't hard to find.

They've all been bought off . . . by the big-money lobbyists and the super-rich campaign contributors who now run the U.S. Government.

And that's a real tragedy – not only for the people who live on the land in Appalachia, but also for the people who used to work there.

Because mountaintop removal doesn't just destroy the landscape; it also destroys mining jobs.

Some background: In the past, the energy company satraps always claimed that they were "providing jobs and helping the economy" – a vitally important fact which they insisted gave them a license to destroy the mountains and valleys that our grandchildren will inherit.

But the "jobs argument" dried up a long time ago. As the statisticians at the U.S. Department of Labor have often pointed out, this new form of "vampire-mining" doesn't actually provide any new jobs.

Instead, it destroys them.

Since 1980, for example, while coal production in West Virginia increased by 140 percent, more than 40,000 coal mining jobs have actually disappeared . . . with perhaps half of them lost to mountaintop removal mining.

The data are frightening enough. But it's even scarier to jump in your car and head for Charleston and regions south . . . where you'll soon find yourself wandering among the new ghost towns and the ruined watersheds of a world we're rapidly bombing back to the Stone Age.

And why are we doing that? The answer is simple.

It's so that the Wall Street moguls who run America's energy industry can "maximize profits" at the expense of the rest of us.

SEVEN

BLOODY BUT UNBOWED

BRIAN HYATT TAKES ON MIGHTY NORTHROP CORPORATION

He's an old man now, and living high above the Pacific Ocean on the island of Maui, and doing his level best to forget what the powerful bosses did to him at the mighty Northrop Corporation, more than 20 years ago.

Brian Hyatt, American whistleblower.

He's trying to forget how they destroyed his career, and took away his livelihood, and left him without an income or a pension or even a chance to catch on with another defense contractor.

They blackballed him, you see? They left him penniless. They left him struggling with depression and a host of physical ailments . . . and wondering how he could pick up the pieces and get on with his broken life. But Brian Hyatt had no choice. He still had children to raise. He had obligations to meet. So he took a deep breath and went to work. Somehow, he managed to pull his world back together and build himself a new business as an entrepreneur who specializes in brokering electronic components internationally for manufacturers all around the globe.

That's what he does today, from his island retreat on Maui.

He survived.

But if you ask 72-year-old Brian Hyatt to describe his feelings about the Northrop Corporation and about the way they treated him after he reported that the huge defense contractor was allegedly cheating the federal government out of tens of millions of dollars each year – while also providing Uncle Sam with defective electronic parts for the vitally important MX Missile – the old man will shake his head and send up a weary sigh.

"You better believe I'm angry, Don," says the astonishingly courageous Hyatt, who took everything that Northrop had to throw at him and then came back for more. "I'm very, very angry. Not just because they tried to destroy me; that goes with the territory, when you're a whistleblower who's going public about contracts that involve millions and millions of dollars. Really, I knew when I decided to speak out against the fraud that there would be reprisals against me, and that they would probably end my career.

"No, I'm angry because of what the executives at the company did to the taxpayers of the United States. To the *citizens* of the United States! They stole millions from the Pentagon, and they basically got away with it. And they supplied the U.S. Pentagon with defective electrical components for the crucially important MX Missile . . . components that they *knew* were flawed, and that might very well have caused that missile to malfunction during an international crisis. And they did this many years before the fall of the Iron Curtain (back in 1989) . . . at a time when the outcome of the Cold War was very much in doubt.

"As far as I'm concerned, when you sell out your country in order to make a profit, you're nothing but a traitor!"

The story of Michael A. "Brian" Hyatt and how he dared to report allegedly corrupt fiscal practices and shoddy workmanship at one of America's largest and most "politically connected" defense firms reads like a thriller straight out of John le Carre. It includes tapped telephones, intercepted mail and even a helicopter circling overhead as Hyatt drove his car one afternoon along a California freeway.

During more than 30 years of counseling whistleblowers, I can't remember meeting one who was more daring – or more determined to speak out against waste, fraud and abuse – than the man you're about to meet. Nor can I think of a better example of "heroism" in our national life.

A SHOCKING DISCOVERY

It began on bright, sunny afternoon in October of 1982, only a few months after a hard-working Senior Microelectronics Process Engineer named Brian Hyatt had signed on at one of America's best-known defense contractors: the Northrop Corporation in Los Angeles.

Hyatt's unit was in charge of making sure that the ceramic-based "hybrid" electrical circuits (used in the guidance system of the MX Missile and other vitally important airborne weapons systems) his people turned out were being properly manufactured – and that they met all of the specifications laid out by the contracts Northrop had earlier signed with the Pentagon.

To understand the huge responsibility this entailed, it helps to know a little bit about Northrop, one of America's most famous and wealthiest defense contractors.

Now known as Northrop Grumman Corporation (after a widely publicized merger in 1994), Hyatt's employer was founded way back in 1939 – and by the early 1980s when he went to work for them, had more than 100,000 employees working at manufacturing sites all around the world. Northrop was a hugely powerful company that earned around $20 billion in gross receipts each year . . . and the California-based enterprise by 1982 had established close contacts in the White House then occupied by their fellow-Californian, Ronald Reagan.

Known worldwide as America's third-largest military contractor (right after Lockheed Martin and Boeing), Northrop would gain almost legendary status as the manufacturer of both the high-tech B-2 Stealth bomber and the F-14 Tomcat made famous by Tom Cruise in the Hollywood blockbuster *Top Gun. The huge Pentagon supplier would also make headlines by gobbling up several other well-known arms-makers, including Litton and TRW, along with that vast DOD manufacturing supplier and builder of destroyers for the U.S. Navy,* Newport News Shipbuilding.

Northrop was a vast, sprawling empire in the early 1980s . . . and yet it's "quality control" procedures were notoriously weak and disorganized. Again and again, the company would be accused of making defective products that were meant to be key components in vitally important U.S. weapons systems. But like the "Teflon President" who'd first been elected in 1980, Northrop had a huge talent for getting away with hanky-panky on a gigantic scale. Like Ronald Reagan, the jumbo-sized arms manufacturer could rest secure in the knowledge that no matter how many violations of the law its corrupt executives might commit, "nothing would stick" . . . and the U.S. Department of Justice would never prosecute.

But then the company made the mistake of hiring Brian Hyatt . . . who soon noticed that something was terribly amiss in the production process that he was supposed to be supervising.

Although the step-by-step manufacturing schedule that Hyatt was monitoring at the Los Angeles plant was technically complex, it can be simply described. In essence, Hyatt and his fellow-engineers were charged with building a series of "hybrid" electronic controllers – circuits that were manufactured micro-miniaturized onto ceramic bases – that would be used to send bursts of information through the MX missiles guidance and propulsion systems. Because the electrical pathways and charges were extremely sensitive and complex, it was essential that the circuits be manufactured with extreme precision.

During the first year or so that Hyatt worked in the unit, the manufacturing process seemed to be working well. Although it took the design team months to set up the specs and then lay out the steps in crafting the internal gold wiring that would run through the circuits, the preparations had gone smoothly, and the team was confident that their product would meet every demand put on it by the missile assemblers working for the Pentagon.

But then a strange problem began to occur.

As Hyatt studied the tiny gold circuits, he noticed that by the end of the production cycle, many were failing an electrical test. With cross-section analysis, he discovered tiny brush-like imperfections that resembled nothing so much as "golden whiskers" that projected through voids in the ceramic, creating "shorts" or "almost shorts" in the internal circuitry.

Hyatt could hardly believe his eyes.

What the hell was going on here?

Unless he was somehow mistaken, the "whiskers" were almost certain to short circuit the flow of current that would be running to the circuit boards, once the current began running through the complex MX Missile wiring scheme.

With a groan of frustration, Hyatt realized the worst: The "whisker" imperfections could not be allowed into the manufacturing process – not without running a significant risk of a breakdown in the electrical distribution, followed by a malfunction of the entire missile. And the results of such a malfunction were unthinkable: what if a warhead-carrying "dummy" device crashed into a neighborhood in the U.S. while being tested? What if a failed MX "Peacekeeper" missile devastated a foreign, non-targeted city? The more he thought about the horrific consequences that might flow from an electrical malfunction, the more alarmed Hyatt became. What should he do? Should he simply agree to "look the other way," like the other engineers in his unit . . . or did he have a responsibility to tell the truth about the potential disaster that lay ahead?

In a flash, Hyatt understood that he was going to have to alert management to the flaws . . . while also insisting that they would have to be corrected. Replacing the "hybrids" would take many months of additional work, and it would probably cost millions of dollars as well.

But what if the brass at Northrop didn't want to take the extra time or spend the extra money?

Oh my God, thought Hyatt. *If I speak out about this problem, I could be putting my neck in the noose! Maybe it would be better to just let the damn things go and pretend I never saw the "whiskers"!*

But he knew he had no choice.

His whole life – as the son of a New York City Civil Engineer who built subways and tunnels and who had refused to allow corrupt contractors to "cheat on concrete" while building the great tunnels that ran under Manhattan and Brooklyn – had prepared him for this confrontation.

He was going to speak out. He was going to tell the truth. And if the brass at Northrop decided to punish him for it . . . then let the chips fall where they might!

Was Brian Hyatt afraid of the retaliation he might face, if he told the U.S. Government and the news media what he knew about the scams that were being run at Northrop? You bet he was, and for good reason: long before he'd arrived on the scene at the company's major manufacturing facility in Los Angeles, the weapons manufacturer had *already* gained a national reputation for playing fast and loose with the laws of the land and then lying about it.

The first real trouble had begun during the early 1970s, when the contract-hungry national defense supplier got caught making illegal campaign contributions to the Nixon administration – along with dispensing a reported $30 million in bribes that Northrop had forked over to foreign governments in order to nail down weapons deals worth billions of dollars. And these unsavory allegations were followed, a few years later, by the disclosure that Northrop executives reportedly staged all-expenses-paid vacations and retreats for Pentagon brass and Congressmen at a posh corporate resort located near the bucolic Maryland seacoast.

And there was more: During the 1980s, even as Brian Hyatt struggled to tell the truth about what was happening in front of his eyes, Northrop would be investigated again and again for mismanaging the production of electronic parts for both the MX missile and the B-2 bomber. In the end, as many journalists and news analysts would report over the years, cheating on contracts was a routine occurrence at Northrop.

Among the culprits, the historical record now shows, was one Clarence Gonsalves – a technician who pled guilty to supervising the falsification of test results on electronic components for cruise missiles and was sentenced to spend three years behind bars as a result.

The record was clear, then, and there could be no doubt: Northrop Corporation in the 1980s was rife with mismanagement, fraud and fiscal abuse. And if *that* was true, then you had to wonder: what *else* were the top brass at the mighty international corporation capable of? How far would they go in order to protect their stolen treasure and their record of malfeasance from prying eyes?

Yes, Brian Hyatt was afraid. (He was *terrified*, in fact . . . as I soon discovered when I agreed to serve as an "expert witness" at his high-profile lawsuit trial during the early 1990s.) But deep down, this bold warrior knew he didn't have a choice. He would risk everything in order to tell the world about the wrongs that were being committed at his workplace, day in and day out.

Years later, a sadly wiser Hyatt would tell me over a cup of coffee in Los Angeles: "I can't believe the way this country has changed during the last 30 years, Don. I mean, after all the sacrifices that were made during the Second World War and the Korean War – to say nothing of the bloody struggle that took place in Vietnam – the thought that American business executives would conspire to cheat their own government by weakening the weapons systems it relies on for national defense is simply beyond my ability to grasp. Try as I might, I can't understand the logic and the lack of values that must be at work when a man decides to betray his country for a lousy dollar.

"I felt the same way after Watergate. You had a president and an administration that had sworn a sacred oath to the U.S. Constitution – and then had gone straight out and done everything they could to *undermine* that same Constitution. When you look at that kind of treachery, you just shake your head and wonder how those Northrop executives could look at themselves in the mirror while they were shaving each morning!"

A LEGACY FROM THE OLD WORLD: "NEVER LIE!"

*So w*hy did Brian Hyatt refuse to remain silent about the corruption he was witnessing daily at Northrop?

Ask the veteran electronics engineer that question, and he won't miss a beat.

"My father escaped from the murderous Cossacks in the old world of the Ukraine," he will tell you with a growl of anger, as he remembers the frequent anti-Jewish "pogroms" that decimated the ghetto community of his ancestors during the first years of the Twentieth Century. "As a boy, he saw Jews running for their lives. He saw a baby speared on the end of a Cossack's saber. He was deeply traumatized, and he knew he had to escape. And he did. Eventually, he made his way to Ellis Island and a new life in America.

"At first he worked as a 'runner' on Wall Street. He knew almost nothing about America. He struggled to learn the language, to learn the culture. Years later, he told us a wonderful story of how he bought a banana for one penny from a pushcart vendor on the street. This was on the Lower East Side. He'd never seen a banana before – and he ate it with the skin still on!"

It was a brutally difficult life at first, but Nathan "Ruben" Hyatt preserved. While working twelve hours a day at starvation wages, he went to Cooper Union College at night in order to learn English and become an engineer. And his endless labor finally paid off: within a few years of arriving in New York, Hyatt Sr. had become a brilliant Civil Engineer who knew how to work with cement and concrete. And he was deeply thrilled, during the 1920s, when he was the responsible engineer at a New York City subway construction site.

But then he discovered that the construction company was cheating on the amount of concrete and reinforcing steel they were using to build the walls of the subway tunnel.

"They were charging the city for all this material and then not using it," Hyatt recalled during a recent interview. "He couldn't believe it. This was his beloved *America* – he couldn't believe that workers would take a chance on safety in order to steal a few extra dollars on the side. So he put his foot down. He approached the supervisors and he told them that he knew what was going on . . . and he demanded that they tear down the portion of the subway that had been built without the necessary concrete and steel.

"Well, the bosses at the construction company couldn't believe this guy was for real. First they offered him money, and he refused to take it. He said, 'No, you'll rip out the bad section and you'll make it right. I'm not going to be part of a crooked deal and then find out a few years from now that the tunnel collapsed and a bunch of people got killed in a subway collapse as a result!'"

The bosses shook their heads in amazement. Then they got down to brass tacks. "They told my father that if he kept their scheme secret, when he retired, they'd have a high-paying job with their company. But he refused to back down. He was astonishingly brave. He went ahead and turned them in – and they went to Sing Sing [a famous New York State prison of that era].

"I never forgot that lesson, you know? And when they tried to intimidate me at Northrop, many years later, I just keep remembering the lesson my dad had taught me while overseeing that subway construction crew. It was the same lesson he had been taught, back in the Ukraine: You must never lie! I followed his example, and when the Northrop bosses set out to destroy me, I clung to the legacy he had left for me.

"It was an honor and a privilege to follow in his footsteps!"

VICIOUS INSULTS BY ANTI-SEMITES

Make no mistake: when Brian Hyatt refused to go along with the cheating on electronic components that was taking place at Northrop in the early and mid-1980s, the bosses did everything they could to humiliate and harass him. "For starters, they yanked me off the floor and stuck me a tiny side office where I was given nothing to do. I had to sit in there all day long and read newspapers and magazines. They took my security clearance and my supervisors would drop by every hour or so to laugh at me.

"They'd stand in the doorway and yell: 'Say, Brian, how do you like your exciting new job? Think you can handle the responsibility? Listen, we think you're doing a great job, reading that newspaper – keep it up!'"

Hyatt did his best to endure the insults, but the reprisals against him were only beginning. As I would later testify (as an "expert witness") during his successful lawsuit for wrongful termination and "infliction of emotional injury," the brass in his department at Northrop soon began resorting to ethnic slurs of the most vicious kind. Again and again, his immediate supervisor would fling a quarter to the floor, then chortle: "Go get it, Brian, that's Jew-bait!" On another occasion, they sent him a birthday card signed "A. Hitler." They made cracks about crafting "lampshades" from his skin. For Hyatt, whose family had been decimated during the Holocaust (several relatives had perished during the brutal 1941 slaughter of nearly 34,000 Jews at Babi Yar in the Ukraine), these anti-Semitic insults were deeply wounding and horrific.

Yet he refused to relent.

"It was pretty painful at times," says Hyatt, who endured several years of harassment and reprisal before finally being fired outright on May 13, 1986. "I got pretty down, and I stared to develop a severe case of clinical depression. But every time I was tempted to throw in the towel and go along with the corrupt practices that were taking place at Northrop, I would remember the example that had been set by my wonderful father. And I would tell myself: Hang on. Don't give up on yourself. Just get through one more day."

Somehow, he managed to keep on going.

It was an amazing thing to watch. When I first interviewed Hyatt – soon after his firing in the mid-1980s – I found it difficult to believe that he was still functioning. As a veteran counselor to whistleblowers, I had seen the devastating impact that speaking out against fraud, waste and abuse usually has on their lives. I had witnessed too many divorces, too many broken homes, and too many descents into alcoholism and paralyzing depression – and I felt fairly certain that Brian Hyatt would end up as they had: a broken man with no job and no hope and no future.

"Don, they're tapping my phones and following me on the street," Hyatt would tell me in a breathless rush, his eyes wild and unfocused. "The other day, they even chased us around L.A. in a helicopter. Believe me, I'm not crazy. Remember: You're not paranoid if they're really out to get you!"

It went on like that, day after day and month after month, and I kept waiting for Hyatt to snap. But he didn't. Instead, he filed the first of several lawsuits . . . even though he knew that Northrop had immense legal resources and *he* had virtually none. (In spite of these enormous odds, however, he actually managed to win a $250,000 settlement against the giant corporation – even though it took him eight years and cost him every penny of his award in lawyers' fees!) He had refused Northrop's multimillion-dollar offer to settle the case before trial.

As the battle heated up and he struggled to find another job in an industry where he was now completely "blackballed," I asked Hyatt again and again why he thought he was managing to survive his whistleblowing ordeal.

"It's simple," he would tell me with his huge, trademark grin. "I've got good genes! How could I *not* stand tall, after the lesson I learned from my father and his father, both of whom were quite willing to risk their lives in order to stand up for the truth and speak out against wrongdoing?"

Brian Hyatt insists that he's not a "religious man." If you press him on his faith, he tell you that he has "no idea whether or not God even exists." He'll also tell you that he knows nothing about the great Old Testament tradition of Jewish prophets like Ezekiel and Jonah and Amos – men who "told it like it was," and who refused to go silent when everybody in their world was telling them to shut up.

"For me, it's not about religion," says Hyatt today. "It's about *blood*. It's about a legacy that I was handed by the people who raised me. And when the crunch came – when I had to put up or shut up – it was that legacy which carried me through the storm."

Actually, this bold whistleblower from sunny California did much more than merely survive.

He *prevailed* – and not only in the courtroom. In one of the most astonishing news reports ever to appear on the celebrated *CBS Sixty Minutes*, Hyatt told the legendary, late Mike Wallace exactly what had gone wrong at the once-invincible Northrop Corporation. After hearing testimony at the House Armed Services Committee, Les Aspin, the Chairman (and later Secretary of Defense), appeared on *60 Minutes* with Hyatt and excoriated the Air Force and Northrop for the numerous frauds that Hyatt had uncovered, along with their subsequent cover-ups. Steven Vales, an agent of the Air Force Office of Special Investigation, also appeared and spoke out against this cover up ... even though the FBI threatened to take his security clearance if he did so.

APRIL 28, 1994: BLOODY BUT UNBOWED!

I spent a few hours hanging out with Brian Hyatt at his gorgeous new home on the Hawaiian island of Maui, and it appeared that life had never been better for this feisty and fearless septuagenarian. Perched high on a majestic hill above the emerald-hued Pacific Ocean, the Hyatt manse is a safe haven caressed by gentle tropical breezes and mellow sunlight. Now a highly successful businessman who ships specialized electronics components all around the world, Hyatt seems to have it all: plenty of money and an island retreat that was the retirement-dream home of a Boeing vice president. And of course, he also enjoys the deeply comforting self-empowerment that comes from knowing he risked everything in order to tell the truth, once upon a time.

Welcome to paradise, Brian Hyatt!

But if you look more closely . . . if you take the time to ask him about the details of his life . . . the picture grows a bit darker. Yes, the Northrop whistleblower *did* manage to survive his ordeal, after being illegally fired and then struggling for more than a decade to find work in an industry that had blackballed him without remorse. And yes ... he did win that California state lawsuit for "wrongful discharge" against mighty Northrop. But the award the jurors gave him turned out to be disappointingly small – not much more than a quarter of a million dollars – and when the expenses and lawyers' fees were finally totaled up, he didn't receive a single dime of the cash the jury had awarded him to make up for the injuries he'd received.

"I could have used that money at the time," Hyatt will tell you today, "but in the end, the lawsuit wasn't really *about* money. It was about me trying to prove in a court of law that what they did to me was illegal and unethical – and on the 28th of April, 1994, I *did* prove that fact, once and for all.

"For me, the decision the court rendered on that day became a beacon of hope. It became a life-sustaining statement of vindication. Really, how can you hope to defeat an enormous international contractor with hundreds of lawyers and endless resources and almost total access to the political system? It's nearly impossible . . . but I did it. I feel that I stood up to them in spite of everything they threw at me, and in the end, I actually prevailed, even with the Department of *In*-Justice working against me."

He shakes your hand and then he sends you his jumbo-sized, signature grin . . . an incredibly courageous truth-teller who went eyeball to eyeball with the very best that corporate America could throw against him . . . and he lived to tell the tale!

Brian Hyatt, American whistleblower.

You have to look closely at his eyes – at the dark shadows that still ring his pain-filled eyes – to understand the price Hyatt paid for speaking out against the fraud that was stealing dollars from the pockets of every taxpayer in America and destroying the effectiveness of our weapons systems.

Yes, his fate is still burning right there in his eyes, and the meaning of his long journey now seems compellingly clear: *Thou shalt not kill the messenger – not if you want America to remain strong and proud and free!*

EIGHT

ROSE GREEN – REQUIEM FOR AN AMERICAN MARTYR

M ost people have never heard of Rose Green, or of the titanic, 14-year battle she fought against the U.S. Library of Congress (LOC).

Suspended and then fired for speaking out against forced "Fitness for Duty" psychiatric exams, she was forced to live without a paycheck or even a due-process hearing for five long years . . . and was then driven into early retirement with no pension to help her face old age or monitor her congenital heart defect.

Punished by merciless federal bureaucrats who remained indifferent to her fate as a whistleblower, Rose Green lost her personal battle for reinstatement at the LOC. Yet she became a hero to the tens of thousands of federal workers who labor daily in government positions managed by the legislative branch. Why? It's simple: Although she couldn't save herself, Rose did manage to alert the U.S. Congress to the loss of rights that can occur when federal workers are required to undergo psychiatric examinations ordered by their bosses.

Reacting to her valiant whistle-blowing, Congress reviewed a forced mental fitness for duty program established by internal LOC regulations and decided to outlaw the exams – thus ensuring that no federal worker in the legislative branch at LOC will ever again have to endure the kind of workplace harassment and humiliation that nearly destroyed Rose's life.

A Very Bad Day at The Office

It began innocently enough, on a raw winter morning on Capitol Hill in the heart of the nation's capital, as Rose piloted her little red car into a parking place.

For the 40-plus-year-old federal worker – a highly experienced attorney in her field who held the title of Assistant General Counsel in OGC Division for the Library of Congress – the day ahead seemed likely to be routine. Moving along briskly, she hurried through a side door and stepped aboard the elevator for the brief ride up to the sixth-floor offices of the Library's Legal Departments.

Once seated in her cubicle on this chilly Friday morning, Rose would begin to review the big stack of procurement contracts that dominated the top of her stainless-steel desk. That detailed and painstaking chore would probably take up most of the long day that loomed ahead. But Rose was actually looking forward to the process; as a veteran lawyer and an expert in federal procurement law who thrived on the complexities of contracting for federal purchases, she enjoyed the intellectual challenge of her job enormously.

Rose had years of experience and training, with plenty of expertise in her specialized fields of administrative law and federal contract law. But as she locked the car and hoisted her briefcase, she felt a sudden surge of anxiety: Uh-oh, what about that meeting with Mr. Jay, the General Counsel (GC), scheduled for late morning?

Previously, Rose had gone to a Congressional oversight committees to discuss the treatment that she was getting regarding an overdue promotion at LOC under the OGC Division 1992 Reorganization plan approved by a Congressional House Budget sub-committee. She had also asked about more office space for pending foot surgery . . . and about not getting fair treatment in general from the Library. Rose had only a tiny open cubicle for work space. She had no office.

After she did this, however, a staffer had called the Library liaison and the word had gotten back to her boss. And now, she feared, the GC had actually set up this meeting in order to retaliate and begin the process of canning her.

Now she sighed unhappily. For the past half-hour or so, as she cruised along the Parkway en route to the office from her home in the suburbs outside Washington, DC, Rose had been able to avoid thinking about today's planned meeting. Instead, she'd been daydreaming pleasantly about her approaching weekend. And why not? She and her artist-husband, Al, a native New Englander and graduate of RISD, had tickets to the Kennedy Center on Saturday night.

But now the pleasurable anticipation she'd been feeling dimmed a bit, as Rose remembered how Mr. Jay, the Library's General Counsel for several decades and her colleague and boss for the past two years, had stuck his head into her cubicle the day before. "Rose," he'd said in a cold, flat voice, "you and I need to talk."

Blinking slowly, she'd looked up at him from the pages of an LOC procurement contract: "We do?"

"Correct," he said. And he wasn't smiling. "Something has come up, regarding the promotion situation, and we need to clear the air a little bit."

She had waited for more but a moment later, he was gone.

What could the problem be? Rose was due for a promotion, no question about that: she was due to move up from GS -905-12 to GS-13, a routine advancement that she fully deserved under the OGC Division 1992 Reorganization.

That promotion was a done deal, wasn't it?

Rose knew it was a done deal under the recent 1992 OGC Division Reorganization, with funding and reorganization structure approved by the Congressional House Budget sub-committee, under which all OGC permanent staff was provided promotion plans for promotion track and advancement. Rose also knew she was expert in her field and that she did good work.

Increasingly worried, she shook her head to clear it. And within a few minutes, the first of the legal contracts she needed to work on was spread out on the desk surface before her. Now she was neck-deep into an analysis of bidding submissions for a new software package that LOC researchers would soon be using to locate materials within the 20 million volumes that made up one of the largest library collections on Planet Earth.

Buried deeply in her legal assessment of the software contracts, Rose hardly noticed the time. And she was genuinely surprised when a shadow suddenly fell over her swivel-chair.

"Rose, it's ten o'clock."

She looked up, startled. Mr. Jay loomed above. Most people who knew him called him simply, "Jay." Round-faced and somber-looking, he did not seem pleased to be greeting her.

"I'm sorry," she said. "Is it ten already?"

But he had turned away and was already striding briskly the few yards back to the door marked: General Counsel.

She followed with her heart in her throat.

A SUDDEN AND SHOCKING REQUEST

Seated in front of Mr. Jay's large and imposing executive desk – he was the top attorney at the world-renowned Library of Congress, after all – Rose struggled to keep her anxiety at bay. With her pulse pounding from the heart palpitations she had experienced since her open-heart surgery, she did her best to maintain a calm, unruffled demeanor.

Rose watched the GC fold his hands together, as if he were about to start praying. She listened as he cleared his throat. Then: "Rose, I might as well go straight to the point. I know you've been concerned about your promotion . . . about the fact that your long-anticipated promotion to GS-13 has not yet occurred."

She stared at him, while an icy current of dread rolled through her midsection. "Well, Jay, I am a little curious about that promotion," she said in low, wavering voice. "As you know, I've been working here in OGC for two years and I have not received performance reviews. And I noticed that all of the other permanent staff attorneys have already received promotions under the 1992 OGC Division Reorganization.

"So yes, I have been wondering a bit . . . when will my own promotion come through?"

His hands were still clasped. For a moment, he reminded her of the evangelical preachers who had ruled the world of her long-ago child-hood in the rural Carolinas. Like Jay, the dour ministers had all worn dark suits and narrow-striped ties. Like her boss, these men of the cloth had spoken in deep, rumbling voices full of unassailable authority. They were figures of enormous power, far off in the distant farmland that had been her struggling girlhood.

He leaned forward intensely now, invading her personal space, and she did her best to look him in the eye.

"Rose, I haven't put in for your promotion, not yet. And I haven't done so for a very simple reason: I don't think you're up to that level."

Rose was confident she was expert in her specialty, government contract and procurement law. She was well trained and experienced in U.S. Government supply, construction, service, intellectual property, computer, and military contracts. Furthermore, she had already served for more than a year as a GS-905-13 Attorney and was eligible for GS-905-14. These were the bases for her qualifications for her legal job at LOC. Her job had actually been formed in response to past procurement controversies at LOC that preceded her arrival at LOC – and she was fully qualified to handle that job.

Rose, with three degrees, was certain she was not just qualified but was *over*-qualified for the GS-905-13 attorney position in OGC at LOC. More exactly, when Rose interviewed for the attorney position in the small OGC Division at LOC, she and her team leader Tony had owned close if not comparable qualifications. The two of them were just one attorney grade level apart in the attorney 905 series. But in less than two years at LOC, while Rose was an experienced woman attorney, Tony – the male team leader who hadn't been a supervisor or manager in the past – had jumped from being only *one* attorney grade-level above Rose to *four* attorney levels above her.

Later, the Chairman of the House Congressional Budget subcommittee with oversight approval of LOC funds for promotions under the 1992 OGC Division Reorganization would learn about this differential in attorney grade levels and would take action to try to correct it.

As the current meeting continued that winter day with the GC, Rose blinked slowly at him, not comprehending his intention "to hold her back" in promotions. "But my performance?"

He was shaking his head. "Performance isn't everything, Rose. There are a lot of other factors, intangible factors that can affect a promotion decision. I don't deny that you've done your work timely – or that you excel in your analysis.

"But I'm concerned about your attitude."

For a moment, she wasn't sure that she'd heard him correctly. "Attitude?" It was nearly a whisper. Her head was whirling now. Her vision had suddenly blurred; for a moment, she feared that she might actually pass out.

Now his round, portly, smug features assembled themselves into a patronizing smirk. "Tony and Karla, new team leaders, questioned your attitude, just last week."

Her heart was hammering so loudly now that she feared it might jump out of her chest. Rose was well aware of the fact that this confrontation was triggering her strong heart palpitations. And that wasn't good for her – because she had been classified medically as "status post open- heart surgery" since her youth, after struggling with a significant congenital heart defect from birth. She was visibly upset now, and the GC knew about her history of heart problems.

"My Team Leader said that about me?"

"He did. And more. He says you've been pushing hard lately for a bigger cubicle."

In a flash, she felt the tears rising to her eyes. "Jay . . . you know I have foot surgery coming up. You know the doctor instructed me to keep my foot elevated and I can't do that in the tiny, closet-size cubicle I work in now. That was a medical request, pure and simple!"

But he was shaking his head. "Tony says you also questioned him as a Team Leader, as a communicator."

"What? That's silly, Jay! All I said was that he never seems to tell you when you've done a good job and he only speaks up when he finds something to criticize. I merely suggested that he might want to take a more positive approach."

Rose knew all this talk about "holding back" her promotions was poppy-cock, in defiance of the terms set out by the Congressional House Budget sub-committee for the 1992 OGC Division Reorganization

– which mandated promotion plans and promotions for the permanent staff. Apparently, the process had been rigged in order to support the hugely generous double promotions which had been granted to the two Team Leaders, Tony and Karla.

But at that moment, the GC snickered out loud. "That's not exactly how Tony described it, Rose. He said you didn't deserve a promotion. Quite frankly he seems to think you're struggling with some personality issues. As a matter of fact, he suggested that you might be able to benefit from some in-house counseling."

Uh-oh. As soon as she heard the word "counseling," Rose stiffened, and for good reason: The Library had for some years used the fitness for duty exam to get rid of employees with employment rights. And now, all at once, she feared that he might be setting her up for the forced fitness for duty exam, where she could be stereotyped as a mental case so that they could use the psychiatrist to do their dirty work.

It wasn't "counseling" that they wanted. This would be a witch hunt designed to attack her and to use the forced fitness for duty exam to end her career. Because it was a known fact in the federal government that if you took an agency-requested psychiatric exam, you would never work again. It was the kiss of death!

Stunned, she gaped openly at him. "Counseling, you say?"

He was scrutinizing her carefully now, and his broad face seemed blank, empty. "Mental health counseling, Rose. Tony, your Team Leader, thinks it might be helpful for you to call the folks over at Employee Services and schedule an appointment with a mental health counselor."

She could hardly believe her ears. "Are you suggesting, Jay, are you actually suggesting that I might have a mental health issue or drug problem?"

He nodded slowly. "I am, Rose. And I think it might be affecting you as an attorney in this office. If you will make an appointment and go over there and speak to someone, I might be able to start the paperwork for your promotion."

For a moment, she felt a ray of hope. Start the paperwork? But then she experienced another wave of dread. All too often, in recent years, she had listened to frightening stories about what happened to LOC employees who opted for mental health counseling at Employee Services. According to the stories, receiving such counseling was professional "suicide." It would result in a black mark that could never be expunged. Once labeled as "crazy" or "alcoholic" by the federal government's mental health counseling staff, an employee would carry that designation in his or her personnel folder all the way to retirement. Although the law prohibited managers from considering mental health issues when making promotions, everybody in Washington knew they did.

How could you trust a worker who had required mental health counseling in the past . . . a worker who might still be mentally unstable?

All at once, Rose realized that she was caught in a trap.

It was the same trap that federal bureaucrats had been using for decades to get at people they didn't like or did not want to promote – or to get at people who spoke up against waste, fraud or abuse in their particular department.

The trap was diabolically simple and terrifying. If the employee refused to seek recommended counseling, the manager would note that fact in the personnel file while also pointing out that this was yet another example of the kind of "uncooperative" and "recalcitrant" behavior that made him or her unfit for promotion.

But if the employee acceded to the request and signed up for the counseling, then the file would carry an ominous warning (between the lines, of course): Be careful before taking on or promoting this worker, who may still be suffering from mental instability!

Rose was caught.

No matter which choice she made, Jay and his allies at LOC would use it against her in order to prevent her future promotions and wreck her life.

With the last of her failing strength, Rose looked her boss in the eye. "Jay, will you give me a day or two to think about it?"

"About getting some psychological counseling, you mean?"

"Correct."

He was already climbing to his feet, and she could see the gleam of triumph in his eye. "Thank you, Rose. I know you'll make the right choice."

IT WAS ALL ABOUT THE PROMOTIONS; IT WAS ALWAYS ABOUT THE PROMOTIONS: ABUSE OF FUNDS AND ABUSE OF POWER

As she drove home later that day to tell her husband about the life-changing career disaster that surely lay ahead, Rose made a valiant decision.

She decided to level with herself.

Insiders at LOC knew the intense history of office politics in LOC's small OGC Division. In the past Jay and Karla, and then Jay, Tony, and Karla had attempted to obtain big promotions . . . first, for Karla, then for Karla and for Tony. The background to all this included tension between Tony and the GC and tension between Tony and Karla.

Tony had worked in LOC OGC his entire career, 25 years since the 1960's. He had resented Karla when she came into OGC in the 1980's, several years prior to Rose, and Karla appeared to surpass him. Likewise, in the 1970's Jay had been chosen as GC over Tony, which chafed Tony. Jay had worked at LOC even longer than Tony, i.e., since law school.

In short, as the result of some crafty political maneuvering and office politics by Jay and Karla, Tony was encouraged to transfer his old resentments from Jay and from Karla – to the new attorney, Rose.

And that was the office politics which Rose stepped into, at OGC in 1991-1992.

One wonders why Mr. Jay, the LOC General Counsel, bothered with these things, since he had in the 1980's been elevated by statute to SES executive level and salary.

In the past Congress had refused to approve the budget for Karla and Tony's big promotions to GS-905-15 or GM-15, behind Jay's big promotion to SES. Congress' response had dominated and controlled the situation.

Then around 1991 the House Budget sub-committee included the restrictions contained in the 1992 OGC Division Reorganization in which Rose's position and qualifications bolstered the reorganization and where promotions and promotion plans were intended by Congress for all career staff in OGC, including Rose's position.

Rose wasn't going to pretend any longer. She wasn't going to kid herself about the real reasons that lay behind Jays insulting refusal to submit the paperwork for her long overdue promotion.

Because the fact was that the General Counsel had awarded promotions to his best buddies in OGC, contrary to what Congress had mandated in the 1992 OGC Division Reorganization at LOC.

The Associate General Counsel Karla had gotten her boost up two levels to the GM-ladder, no questions asked.

Tony had gotten his double promotions, you could be sure of that.

Everyone except Rose had received their promotions so she wrote a letter requesting Jay's attention to this matter of her promotion.

Tony may have been the only attorney promoted in the federal government to a GM-905-15 without prior management experience. He was probably the single government attorney promoted at that time to GM-905-15 to supervise no one or at most only one or two GS-11 or 12 Attorneys.

Rose only hoped as a woman attorney she would be granted the same benefit of the doubt Tony had enjoyed as the male attorney on her team, whenever her turn came up for rapid, double promotions to GM-905-15!

Rose had already served as a GS-905-13 Attorney and was qualified for GS-905-14 level attorney. Ironically, her career position in OGC with skills and qualifications were used to support the team structure and reorganization for Tony and Karla's huge promotions, plus her employment at LOC. Recalling this was a poignant matter.

Truth was, despite her status and expertise as a woman attorney, Jay and his allies were pushing Rose under the bus. They were blocking her first promotions mandated under the 1992 OGC Division Reorganization to even a level she already held, GS-905-13. They were doing this after using Rose to obtain their own double promotions and huge salary increases. Without Rose's career attorney status in OGC at a level high enough to support GM-905-15 positions, their promotions were suspect.

Jay, Tony, Karla, and allies had used Rose as a career employee in the team structure to promote Tony and Karla as attorneys, times two. They persisted in distorting the requirements of the OGC Reorganization – the terms and funding – by taking the funds and advancement for themselves as attorneys. They used Rose Green and then excluded her from the benefits of the OGC Division 1992 Reorganization.

In short, Jay, Karla, and Tony set out to do what they had planned all along, prior to the 1992 OGC Reorganization. They obtained big promotions and salary increases for themselves, i.e., for Karla and for Tony. They achieved it by ignoring Congress' requirements to implement Congress' terms in the 1992 OGC Division Reorganization – promotion plans and promotion schedules for all career, permanent staff in OGC.

Jay and his allies stomped on the Congressional terms and destroyed Rose's career to obtain their coveted advancements. They did this when the funding for promotions for all career staff, including Rose, was already provided. Karla and Tony wanted and achieved advancement exclusively for themselves as attorneys, just as Jay had requested from Congress in prior years and been denied. Again, this was exactly what Congress in the past refused to approve for funding for advancement, promotions, and salary increases for Karla and then for Tony.

Years later, in the next century, as a gratuity to Tony during a hearing, Rose was formally asked to explain why she should have been promoted, considering Tony's years of service at LOC.

Rose's whistle-blowing case wasn't just about the broad abuse of power by LOC, an Internist, the GC, his allies, and Psychiatrists with a "gulag" mentality or about the forced mental exam process that had been established to deny basic due process rights and to deny equal protection of career staff employees (including EEO civil rights). Nor was it only about the later denial of rights under the 1991 ADA – and later still, the denial of changes in the 1995 LCRs as they affected Rose in her case.

No, the whistle blowing was also about abuse of federal funds by the LOC, GC, Internist, Psychiatrists, Personnel Office, and Jay's other allies, especially by Tony and Karla, when they all employed the forced FFD process to distort the terms and use of federal funds provided by Congress and the House Budget sub-committee for all promotions under the 1992 OGC Division Reorganization.

Rose has long wondered what lay behind Jay's ruthless campaigns for two others – for the huge promotions for Karla & Tony. Since Jay was already SES executive level by statute, one might say he had no dog in that fight for promotions below himself.

PLUNGING INTO "THE SHEER HELL" OF WHISTLE-BLOWING

As Rose pulled her compact car into her garage outside Washington, D.C. she was already devising the desperate strategy that she knew she would need in the days ahead.

Yes, she would make the call to Employee Services, and she would visit their offices down on the second floor for the "employment counseling" that Jay seemed to think she needed. But she would also make a few other calls, starting bright and early on Monday morning.

One of those calls would be to the internal EEO office at LOC, where she would ask about the steps involved in filing a formal complaint alleging "gender discrimination and hostile work environment in the workplace."

Another call would go to one of her contacts on Capitol Hill, a congressional staffer whom she trusted at the House of Representatives Budget sub-committee.

Suddenly, the unthinkable was looming on the horizon: Rose, from a small-town in the South who had done what her bosses had asked of her, was about to start "going public" about the rampant favoritism and the ugly civil rights violations that were taking place at the Library of Congress.

Rose was going to become a whistleblower.

What followed that momentous decision was a violent plunge into what Rose would later describe as sheer hell. It would be a nightmare – the brutally vindictive and psychologically paralyzing world of those who decide to stand up and speak out about waste, fraud and abuse in the federal government.

During the agonizing 14-year battle that was beginning, she would experience many of the extraordinary highs and lows that take place daily in the rollercoaster-like lives of American truth-tellers.

Again and again, Rose's tortured odyssey through the perilous world of whistle-blowing would illustrate how this deeply traumatic experience affects human beings, and how it permanently transforms their lives.

Writing some years ago in *Psychology Today* magazine, I outlined the "Seven Stages" that typically occur during that odyssey. I also described their devastating emotional impact on most whistleblowers, as follows:

1. Discovery. Anger, shock and a sense of betrayal are common, particularly if the employee has unwittingly assisted the fraud, waste or other corruption. Many prolong the discovery state by denying it.

2. Reflection. During this period, individuals weigh the consequences of silence versus speaking out. For some, the prospect of confronting another even anonymously is so threatening that they cannot sleep. Fear is heightened for those who anticipate trouble or for those who lack a sense of direction. Many suffer alone and become obsessed with the problem. Others try to break the tension by acting too quickly, leading to hasty, ineffective actions that cause problems later.

3. Confrontation. Once a decision is made, the stress of anticipation is over. Now whistleblowers experience the strain of revealing their charges. If they have acted openly, they may fear retaliation. If they have done it covertly, they worry about being found out.

4. Retaliation. This can take many forms, ranging from threats to slander and economic reprisals. Most retaliation is designed to threaten whistleblowers into backing off or to discredit their testimony. Few people are prepared to handle retaliation, particularly if friends and colleagues abandon them when the going gets tough. Many feel like outcasts. An engineer reported that "even though your charges are proved true, you're treated like a leper." A man who caught a college

president embezzling said that other faculty members stopped speaking to him. A woman who uncovered extensive fraud in a defense contractor's office watched friends she had counted on as witnesses bought off one by one with promotions, while she was blackballed from other jobs within the industry.

5. The long haul. In the months and years between confrontation and resolution, stresses may intensify. Since the burden of proof usually falls on whistleblowers, legal bills may mount rapidly. If they have been fired, they may be heavily in debt and face the loss of home, spouse, children, car, friends and everything else. At times whistleblowers are swamped with hearings, depositions and other legal activities; at other times, as their case stalls, they fear that all their risks have been in vain. Righteous fury can easily tip into obsession, costing whistleblowers whatever friends and supporters they have left. Without professional assistance, and a lot of luck, many whistleblowers never move beyond this stage.

6. Closure. Eventually the case is won or lost or the whistleblower stops pursuing it. There is a feeling of relief combined with pain if the outcome is unsatisfactory. For most whistleblowers, a period of mourning is necessary.

7. Resolution. Final acceptance may come with closure. Or it may take many years to fully appreciate what has happened, to understand it and to feel healed. Some whistleblowers never reach this stage.

THE GC LAWYER, THE DOCTOR INTERNIST, AND THE FIRST PSYCHIATRIST

In the past Jay, the GC, had shared with Rose his view about employees' medical records. He discussed with her his opposition to employees' access to their own medical records.

As Rose gasped to herself and wondered why Jay had forgotten he went to law school, she realized that many bureaucrats could be counted to have access to employee private medical records – but not the employee!

In time Rose came to understand, as with Jay, how he would from time to time speak about his alliance with Sheila George, M.D.,

Internist, who was recruited in the 1980's as chief of Medical Services Division at LOC. She had immigrated to the U.S. for medical school with a specialty in Internal Medicine. Despite her lack of clinical work or specialty in mental health, she was also appointed chair of the forced FFD Committees at LOC.

This alliance was rounded out with Dr. Roy Book, a local psychiatrist with specialty in drug abuse cases.

In time, Rose, an attorney who held a Masters in Public Health degree, questioned if Dr. George believed the Hippocratic Oath applied to her.

Jay was apparently so involved in the politics at LOC that Rose wondered how he had time to practice law. Eventually Rose put the history together. Dr. George, the Internist, was not just appointed to the Committee position. The Internist was recruited from a hospital where she worked in medical records.

Before the Internist Dr. George's arrival at LOC, few employees had been taken to task for emotional, mental or alcohol problems.

With their alliance beginning in the 1980's – the GC and the Internist – LCR (or Library Regulations) were passed establishing a forced mental fitness for duty process and committees to label career staff employees at LOC with mental labels and then transfer, terminate, or force them into retirement.

In this process, again and again, due process and procedural rights as well as rights under the ADA were denied, ranging from no standards for charges, evaluations, findings, or punishment to denial of proper notice and hearings to labeling employees with perceived disabilities in violation of the ADA.

Not to mention the layers of equal-protections problems involved with the employees targeted by the process. And the fact that the entire scheme was established to avert career staff employees' rights to be protected from termination, transfer, or retirement without cause – and to be protected from other discrimination – seemed to count for little. Plus the scheme was later maintained in violation of the 1991 ADA.

In Rose's case she was slandered as a professional and her property rights to use her license were damaged.

So the Internist was recruited and the doctor and the GC lawyer connived and contrived to put together a program that would pursue other employees and naturally exclude themselves, since Jay was famous for his outrageous temper.

A review of the dozens of employees subjected to the abuses showed that managers and supervisors at LOC were excluded. They were not pursued. The process would deny career staff employees equal protection as well as basic notice, due process, procedures, and standards, and apply perceived medical labels to them as in a Russian Gulag, contrary to both the ADA and federal rules since 1984.

Numerous times Rose tallied alliances by Jay and the Internist. For example, Jay coordinated with Dr. George to follow Rose into the LOC parking garage when Rose was in a rush to prepare for her foot surgery. Jay set Rose up by delaying and frustrating her upstairs and then sending Dr. George to follow Rose. Dr. George then claimed Rose tried to use her small compact car to hit her Mercedes in the garage. Instead of reporting this to the police, the GC and Internist concealed a report for six months so it would not be easy for Rose to recall the details later, after her surgery.

Jay, the GC, and Dr. George, the Internist, were great allies and harmed other people contrary to their training and the oaths of their professions. It was also shocking that Jay claimed to be a very religious, devout Catholic. Sadly, both the GC and the Internist continued to retain their licenses to practice in the U.S. despite their conduct at LOC.

The LOC forced FFD process was set up and carried out by them despite the changes made by Congress and the Executive Branch in 1984 to cease forced mental exams on employees where they were not required in their position descriptions, such as for police and pilots.

In another huge denial of equal protection, the scheme was applied and used only on LOC career staff employees and not on LOC managers and supervisors. And the scheme was applied despite the demands of the ADA since 1991. And they were applied unequally among staff employees because there were no standards for any part of the process – charges, exams, findings, or punishment. It was set up to take action against some career staff employees by labeling them and forcing them to transfer, retire, or terminate without cause.

As standing members, Dr. George the Internist and Dr. Book the Psychiatrist, filled out part of the voting panel for forced mental Fitness for Duty Committees which they would proceed to use on several dozen career staff employees into the 1990's. Their victims included a woman with a possible case of agoraphobia.

The other members of each ad hoc FFD Committee were lay persons. They were various managers plus human resources personnel who wanted to force termination, transfer, or retirement without cause. They did not have experience in mental health care. These voting members were all lay (not mental health) persons on the FFD Committee but for the in-house psychiatrist who specialized in drug abuse and alcohol cases. The LOC process was totally devoid of due process and was used to transfer, terminate, or retire career staff employees when LOC did not otherwise have cause to do so.

Again, it is noted that the LOC forced mental FFD process was a dastardly process, not used against managers and supervisors but only against career staff employees. Apparently, according to Dr. George and LOC, managers and supervisors didn't have mental health issues or drinking problems.

For example, Jay, the GC, who sported a blistering temper with full-blown temper tantrums at work, was a voting member of the forced FFD Committee against Rose, despite her history of complaints of discrimination and harassment against Jay and his office.

So the LOC forced mental FFD process was fraught with many problems – due process, procedural, equal protection. No standards even existed for carrying it out: Charging, labeling, examining, findings, application of findings, punishment, were all subject to abuse of process and abuse of power.

Dr. George and management did what they wanted to do. One might ask if LOC was part of a banana republic? An employee was terminated as late as 2001 with the use of this LOC forced FFD Committee process despite Congress' attempt to intervene in 1995. Even after Congress' Joint Committee on the Library wrote to the Library in summer 1995 to alter the forced FFD Regulations at LOC, Dr. George and the Library continued after 1995 to make up more severe forced FFD panels and exams against some employees without Regulatory authority.

That was part of the terrible history of forced medical and mental labeling at LOC under the alliance of the GC and the Internist – even beyond Congress' passage and application of the ADA specifically to the Library of Congress in 1991 and beyond the initiative to change LOC Regulations in 1995 – and all of this occurred after Congress' other initiatives in this area, dating back to 1984.

HOSTILE WORK ENVIRONMENT, HARASSMENT, RETALIATION — HELL

It is noted that after the onset of promotions in summer and fall of 1992 under the 1992 OGC Division Reorganization, only weeks later, Rose Green was pressured to see an LOC in-house shrink, Dr. Roy Book, Psychiatrist and proclaimed drug specialist.

He claimed expertise in drug abuse and alcohol cases and had a private office on Old Georgetown Road in Bethesda, Maryland. Employees referred to him as the Library's "hired gun" who according to Rose was paid to find whatever the Library wanted in their exams. He was also a standing member of LOC's forced mental FFD Committees.

When this happened, Rose was not advised that she was being evaluated to transfer, retire, or terminate her from her attorney position – only weeks after the promotion plans went into effect under the 1992 OGC Division Reorganization. Nevertheless, she received a favorable report.

This was initiated against Rose to try to block her eligibility for attorney promotions under the 1992 OGC Division Reorganization. Her father was dying at the time. She had foot pain and needed foot surgery. Plus she'd had heart palpitations since her birth defect and major heart surgery. And her boss was trying to block her promotions.

Since the Library could not get the desired report from the in-house doctor to exclude her from her attorney position in OGC at that time, Jay and his allies changed to Plan "B" which meant increasingly "hostile work environment" with harassment and retaliation between 1992 and 1994. In other words, they tried to frustrate and drive her crazy. This forced Rose to consult with the internal Library EEO office and with the Congressional House Budget sub-committee in 1993 to seek resolutions.

To quote Rose Green, she "never knew hell until [she] went to EEO and Congress!"

What followed Rose's decision to file a formal LOC EEO complaint of discrimination in the federal workplace is painful to relate. And if you had to choose a single word to describe the sequence of events that soon followed that decision, the operative word would probably be: Nightmare.

"The reprisals began within a matter of hours," Rose would tell me later, as she sat weeping in my office in suburban Maryland. "For starters, I was told that since I was not 'a good team player,' I would be excluded from all decision-making meetings and policy reviews, starting immediately."

At work Rose Green was reduced to answering the phones with three degrees while the clerk in OGC studied for her first degree, which was also paid for by the Library.

"Henceforth, the Library threatened to assign me to an even smaller cubicle, located far down a distant hallway and I would not have my job."

They talked about sending Rose to another building and changing her position description so she would not qualify for attorney promotions under the 1992 OGC Division Reorganization.

The continuing legal education courses earned by each attorney were all but eliminated for her. Then they threatened to transfer her out of OGC and her attorney position, which was equivalent to a demotion.

"Being exiled from the day-to-day operations of the LOC OGC Division was bad enough," she remembers. "But the hardest part of the ordeal was the insulting and humiliating treatment I received from my bosses and co-workers. Once I 'went public' by contacting the EEO at LOC – along with alerting a Congressional staffer who then wrote a letter demanding that Jay explain why I hadn't been promoted – the other people in my department began to treat me like a leper."

Rose' foot surgery was delayed until late 1993 due to the perennial harassment. Shortly after she returned from foot surgery in late 1993, she and Jay were the last two employees to depart the Division office.

After Jay left, Rose found a very large, ugly plastic rodent on the cabinet in her tiny cubicle. This frightened her. She was being called a "rat" and she felt threatened.

For more than a decade as the principle party against Rose, Jay spit at her, clinched his fists and struck her, ridiculed and confined her, and held back her advancements, yet he never once provided a sworn statement.

As the weeks turned into months and the war of nerves continued at the LOC, Rose grew increasingly depressed and exhausted. Afflicted since birth with a heart defect that can leave her with heart palpitations at times, she was sinking into the dark labyrinth of sadness and despair that so often disables whistleblowers during what I have described as "The Long Haul" (see above) period of the typical whistle-blowing experience.

Eyeball to Eyeball with More Psychiatrists and Psychologists

Incredibly, the "nightmare" dragged on and on into 1994 when Jay or GC & Co. suddenly switched tactics. Resorting to an outdated (and clearly unethical) LCR or LOC regulation, a rule that had already been outlawed throughout the executive branch of the federal government (see Chapter 1 for a description of the Wilma Jefferson case and how it resulted in the prohibition of forced fitness for duty psychiatric exams in all federal government executive agencies), the GC & Co. (Jay and his allies) at the LOC demanded that Rose submit to a forced FFD exam.

When Rose first knocked on my office door in the late winter of 1994, I quickly reassured her that she had some important "due process" rights in the matter of the FFD exams. I also promised to accompany her to any and all forced psychiatric exams that she might be required to undergo.

I kept that promise a few months later – several times. According to Rose, before she (Rose) met with each doctor, the LOC medical chief,

Dr. Sheila George, Internist, briefed each doctor on what she and Jay wanted. Dr. George, chairperson of the forced FFD committee, instructed the doctors to steer clear of her history of birth defect and childhood handicaps so that meant staying away from her childhood stresses and the similar bullying she had experienced as a child with handicaps.

Rose also had as a child the fear of dying since some other children she knew with heart defects died young. She also suffered from survivors' guilt about their deaths. She felt committed to doing something significant and becoming a woman attorney since her childhood friend died very young following heart surgery. None of these things were explored. They were avoided like the plague because Dr. George, Jay and the FFD Committee blocked them.

Especially excluded was the parallel bullying that Rose experienced in her OGC office employment and as a handicapped child. The doctors were also instructed to omit any parallel discussions about how it felt for Rose to be labeled with a pile-on of medical labels after she endured medical labels since birth and as a handicapped child. Or how it felt for everything she worked for as a handicapped woman who grew up on a farm to be taken away, as it was proposed to remove Rose from her attorney position (and future promotions as an attorney) – when Rose, a Christian, was called in to hear this news on the eve of the Christmas holidays, Thursday afternoon, December 23, 1993.

All this was avoided and excluded by the hired doctors so they could not do a complete interview or exam. They could not look at what it meant to Rose as a handicapped woman to become one of the first attorneys in the 1970's. They also could not look at the parallel between the bullying at work and the bullying she was conditioned to as a handicapped child. They also misinterpreted Rose's heart palpitations. This meant a distorted review and report from each doctor.

When Rose arrived for her forced psychiatric exam at a doctor's office in Washington, I stood at her side carrying a yellow legal pad and a ball-point pen. Startled by my presence, the male psychiatrist stared at me as if I'd just arrived on the scene from Planet Mars.

"Who are you?" he asked, probably assuming I was a lawyer who'd blundered into his office in the mistaken belief that he would be allowed to sit in on a private medical exam.

"I'm Dr. Don Soeken. I'm a licensed clinical social worker, and Rose is my patient. And before we get started, I should also inform you that I regard this examination as unethical.

"Doctor, are you aware that these forced fitness for duty exams have already been prohibited by statute in the executive branch of government since they clearly and obviously violate the rights of the federal workers who are illegally subjected to them?"

The psychiatrist was glaring at me even harder now. "I should also point out," I continued in a controlled concerned tone, "Rose may be accompanied during the exam by a properly licensed mental health counselor."

I'll never know if it was my note-taking presence that caused the psychiatrist to have a change of heart that day, but the fact is that after interviewing Rose and asking her many questions, he later announced that he was withdrawing from the case entirely, and he did!

Undeterred, however, the LOC and the GC hired another shrink to conduct another exam.

Undismayed, I reached once again for my yellow legal pad. Once again, I made my little speech about the "unethical and illegal" character of these forced exams.

Amazingly enough, the third psychiatrist also withdrew from the process, after she conducted a two-hour preliminary interview with the embattled Rose. Was it my yellow legal pad, I later wondered – or did the doctor make a deal with Dr. George, the chairperson of the LOC Fitness for Duty Committee, to provide statements later without completing an examination?

The fourth examination of Rose was ordered by LOC after she was suspended – and after the LOC Regulations per forced mental FFD examinations were changed in 1995 at the behest of Congress in summer 1995. LOC abandoned all rules; indeed, they had no rules. They ordered Rose Green to attend a whole panel of doctors – psychiatrists and psychologists at one time – regardless of the stress this might cause. Even the criminally insane are not treated or examined in this manner.

It didn't end there, however; after she filed her case the Federal court judge ordered a fifth examination by an independent medical examiner (IME) – nearly 10 years after her working at LOC – but this psychiatrist completed one exam or interview, required written testing, and gave no diagnosis. That psychiatrist did not allow me in the room when she did the testing. or interviews. The doctor did not diagnosis her and one can assume that the doctor did not find any mental disorders.

The value of a mental exam 10 years after employment is questionable but clearly Rose's case had become about the fabricated charges brought by the government. Her case was not about her charges of EEO or ADA discrimination. Her charges were never heard.

The sixth psychiatrist who examined Rose was hired by her as a consultant. He was a respected expert in fitness for duty exams as well as criminal cases. Dr. Roberts found that Rose was fit for duty and did not have a diagnosis of mental illness.

SUSPENSION, REGULATIONS AND CONGRESS

Despite all the medical exams that found not a scintilla of evidence to diagnose a mental illness, Rose's luck ran out on February 15, 1995. The GC-led allies at LOC informed her that she had just been "suspended from her job" – without pay – since she was "not an acceptable risk in the workplace." When they came to her cubicle to tell her, they threatened her with a weapon (gun), if she tried to get her things to take with her.

This bogus charge was without merit and was an arbitrarily deceitful decision that took the career of a dedicated civil servant who followed the Code of Ethics of Government Service.

Rose explained that she had spent much of her life studying government and law, only to be put down.

Before Rose was suspended, she was subjected to what is called "bifurcated" charges. Then, she was not provided a copy of all the internal administrative decisions made regarding those charges against her despite repeated requests. These procedural and due process errors by the Library went on and on in her case.

Even after Rose was suspended, she was pursued by the GC & LOC for years. She was left in limbo, slandered, and with no pay and no due process hearing for more than five years. Rose Green was never given the benefit of the changed LOC Regulations (LCRs) called for by Congress and issued in 1995 for non-union employees, although her termination was not proposed for years and then not processed until 2001.

In attempting to help Rose I decided to go to the Library of Congress Unions to determine whether the psychiatric exams were used on anyone else. I could not believe it when I found that it was a routine procedure that the library had used many times on non-managers since Dr. George joined LOC.

So I asked the union representative to provide me with a list of cases, but without the names. He supplied me with 35 cases, and I sent a letter that contained the list to Senator Connie Mack, who reviewed the information. We also got the press involved and several articles appeared in the Congressional Quarterly, written by Juliet Alpern, who investigated and reported on the whole process.

Senator Mack and other Senators and Congressmen investigated and held hearings after reviewing the documents. They demanded more information from LOC; however, data on any case like Rose's was excluded. In 1995 Congress' Joint Committee on the Library prompted the Library of Congress to change their rules and regulations so that all regulations passed by Congress in 1984 were to apply equally to all LOC employees.

Rose was never given the benefit of the changed LOC 1995 LCR Regulations pertaining to the forced FFD process. The old regulations and worse were applied to Rose in all future years, as the sacrifice for exposing and ending this abusive process.

JUSTICE IN AMERICA – OR IS IT "JUST US"?

Rose finally received a hearing in her case by a hearing officer outside LOC more than five years later in 2001, after which the hearing officer issued a decision recommending that Rose be reinstated with full benefits. The Library, after this five-year suspension without pay and benefits, ignored the hearing officer's decision and recommendations. The Library terminated Rose Green. Worst of all, LOC provided no reasons or basis for termination after Rose waited 5 years for an administrative hearing outside LOC.

Failure to provide notice of reasons and good reasons for termination is a major DP (due process) violation. This forced Rose Green to file in federal court, which cost her and her attorney many thousands of dollars.

After she filed her case the federal court judge ordered a fifth examination, an independent medical exam (IME) which was requested and paid for by the Library of Congress. The relevancy of an exam and report nearly 10 years after Rose worked at LOC is doubtful yet she had to endure the abuse. The Psychiatrist completed the exam and did not give a diagnosis. The doctor did not diagnose her and one can assume that the doctor did not find any mental disorders.

This process exposed Rose to further property damage involving the use of her license.

Rose's charges of EEO and ADA discrimination were ignored.

So what did the judge base his opinion on? Apparently, in his court he converted the decade-old charge against Rose from a medical charge to a conduct charge. He treated it as a conduct charge.

This presented a 10-year old DP problem – lack of notice of the charges – against Rose for a decade and led to her fighting the wrong charge for a decade.

In another distorted twist of U.S. employment law, the federal judge in Rose's case upheld her termination for an alleged first offense, which is against all trends in American employment case law.

To fire an employee for an alleged first offense goes to the severity of punishment and is not supported in case law.

Rose eventually lost because the federal judge dismissed her case in the end without any diagnosis or mental disability – in a case where her boss had struck her, spit at her, and threatened her – and in a case where she was harassed and retaliated against after being eligible for promotions and complaining. In short: the Library had won on false pretenses.

In the end, the judge decided Rose could be fired without cause and without due process rights, although she had been a permanent employee for many years and treated as a permanent employee.

It is basic that employees without job rights are terminated summarily and not subjected to protracted, "for cause" procedures. An employee with job rights would receive due process and procedural protections. It is one or the other. An employee at the Library of Congress is one or the other – with or without job rights. Special testing is provided for only in a position description such as for police and pilots.

The upshot is that all employees subjected to a mental fitness for duty exam must be afforded due process. The courts need to make this clear to protect American workers. Due process is imperative.

Rose even underwent a Reduction-in-Force (RIF) while employed in the small OGC Division at LOC during which she was treated as a permanent employee by OGC and LOC.

Congress and LOC also treated Rose as a permanent employee regarding promotions under the 1992 OGC Division Reorganization. Indeed, it was required under the reorganization to support the weighty, double promotions obtained by Tony and Karla.

During all of Rose's employment with LOC she was treated as a permanent employee. LOC and the U.S. Attorneys did not raise the issue as an issue or defense when she filed in federal court.

Apparently, the judge misrepresented Rose's career status in order to circumvent the mountain of procedural and DP errors by LOC and to distort the other legal issues – EEO, ADA – to give him an avenue to find in favor of LOC and the government.

In turn, these misrepresentations were used to distort the outcome in the case. It is noted that this federal judge in the past was given an award from LOC and should have disclosed this and notified every party in the case in order to recuse himself or offer to recuse himself. However, the Judge ruled despite the apparent conflict of interest while he concealed or failed to disclose.

That same federal district judge in Rose's case went further. He offered to conceal his decision against Rose in her case from publication if, of course, she waived her right to an appeal and agreed not to appeal. Such bartering by a judge was unseemly.

According to Rose, each attorney involved in her case concealed the truth that she was indeed a permanent career LOC employee. She also contends that each attorney involved perpetrated a fraud on the court, including Mr. Jay, long-time GC, who is still licensed although retired. Tony, Karla, and all the U.S. Attorneys, because they knew and had the evidence to show that Rose was indeed a permanent career LOC employee.

All these attorneys who call themselves officers of the court – including the federal judge, Mr. Jay, and all the other government attorneys at LOC and the U.S. Attorney's Office – lied and fabricated an excuse in order to get out of awarding Rose her rightful decision in her case and return to her job with benefits – and in order to find for LOC and the government.

It remains to be seen if Mr. Jay, GC at LOC for many years, has or will come forward and tell the truth with statements about Rose's career status and, therefore, will shed light on her rights to due process and equal protection.

Especially since the GC was the official who attested to Rose's permanent career status in 1991 when she was hired.

It also remains to be seen if Jay has or will ever come forward and tell the truth with sworn statements and allow Rose's name to be cleared in her lifetime.

YES, ABUSE OF POWER AND ABUSE OF FUNDS

During all the years of this continuing workplace struggle, however, neither Jay nor any of his lieutenants and allies has ever successfully explained why Rose was "not an acceptable risk." Reserved and often soft-spoken, and quiet at times, Rose endured a hostile work environment not unlike the childhood bullying she absorbed in her youth as a handicapped child with a congenital birth defect. Her boss Jay spit at her, clinched his fists at her, threatened her job, and struck her; he harassed her and retaliated after she filed complaints.

Reviewing the record in detail as I have more than once, you have to wonder if it was actually her penchant for telling the truth that got her into trouble with her bosses at the LOC, along with her EEO & ADA complaints about promotions in OGC, her surgery, and the work environment.

Increasingly ill, her parents died and her artist-husband Al died of an asthma-related ailment. These days, Rose soldiers on alone, a sad widow who wishes to revive public interest in her legal case against the world-renowned U.S. Library of Congress.

Looking back at that case, it now seems clear that Rose has not yet reached the final "Resolution" stage that many whistle-blowers eventually achieve. Although she lost her legal case and paid a terribly high personal price for blowing the whistle on duplicity and discrimination in the federal workplace, and for blowing the whistle on abuse of power and abuse of funds, Rose did not suffer in vain.

Why? Because her long struggle for a measure of justice actually produced some results of major significance in the continuing battle for human rights in this great country of ours.

After I presented her incredibly painful story along with massive documentation to former U.S. Florida Republican Senator Cornelius McGillicuddy III (known popularly as "Connie Mack"), who had always been an empathetic supporter of federal employees, the Sunshine State lawmaker took it upon himself to lead a year-long campaign to force the LOC to discontinue their illegal and misguided policy of forced fitness for duty exams against new and more employees.

After that, Dr. George the Internist and Mr. Jay the GC left LOC. The LCR regulation now assures that forced fitness for duty exams will never again be foisted on employees who work for the legislative branch of the U.S. Government if it is not provided for in the position description – as set by example at the Library of Congress. For helping us to achieve that one single step, Rose has my deepest and heartfelt thanks.

As I often have noted during media interviews and seminars on the dynamics of whistle-blowing in the government workplace, Rose deserves the deepest respect and also the undying gratitude of Americans everywhere who value our protected liberties and wish to prevent a "gulag" from emerging in our own government.

Rose was a true American martyr for the cause of personal freedom. She stood tall again and again for our deepest values and her shining legacy of personal courage and spiritual valor will continue to inspire all those who love liberty, far down into the 21st Century and beyond!

NINE

RUSSELL TICE: BLOWING THE WHISTLE

ON THE WORLD'S LARGEST SPY AGENCY

Russell Tice was in the middle of a sentence ... when all at once his expression changed.

Suddenly, his greenish-brown eyes were full of suspicion.

"Look over there," said the former National Security Agency (NSA) intelligence analyst. "See that guy sitting beside the fireplace? That guy was just sitting at the computer over there – and then he left and came back with a laptop! Why did he need a laptop, if he was just using the *other* computer? That behavior looks kind of suspicious to me."

Now he was keeping a close eye on the man on the other side of the lobby of the Marriott Garden Court Hotel, located in Maryland on the outskirts of Washington, D.C. Eyes narrowed; Tice was carefully watching the tall, slender man in the neatly pressed, charcoal-gray suit.

"That's a pattern of behavior I've witnessed in many FBI agents," he said after a bit. "I've been followed many times in the past, and I've learned how these agents operate. Not long ago, my wife and I went out to dinner. We're sitting at a back table, and all at once we've got company. It's *another* FBI agent, and he's just taken up residence at a table near ours. In the near empty restaurant, without having the hostess seat him

"It's a familiar pattern," said the nationally renowned whistleblower, a powerfully built, former college football player at defensive end who'd made front-page news a few years before, when he went public with the shocking disclosure that the giant spy agency – his employer, the National Security Agency– was illegally spying on millions of American citizens.

"We can't talk here," Tice said now. "Look – he isn't navigating any pages on his laptop, and he's not doing anything with the hotel computer, either. That tells me something . . . and I'm not comfortable talking about these issues with him sitting so nearby."

The former spook was on his feet now, and headed toward the massive oaken doors that opened onto the Marriott parking lot. "If it's okay with you," said Russell Tice, "it might be better to do the rest of this interview in your room."

This is the world that Russell Tice inhabits – a dark, shadowy world full of phone taps and hidden electronic bugs and high-tech instruments that can send intelligence racing across thousands of miles of space in a fraction of a second.

Living in that world, permanently, is the price he pays for having told the truth about the law-breaking he says he witnessed a few years ago at the world's largest intelligence agency, the NSA.

Tice's stunning message: The highly vaunted NSA, often praised as the best and most effective intelligence-gathering organization on Planet Earth, has been routinely violating the Constitutional rights of millions of American citizens – throughout much of the past decade.

If you want to understand the extraordinary secrecy within which NSA operates, ask yourself what at first might seem to be a routine and innocuous question:

Q. How many people work at NSA?

The answer, you may be surprised to learn, is: *Sorry, that's classified.*

Ever wondered how many tax dollars go into the annual budget that supports the jumbo-sized spy agency each year? The answer, of course: *Sorry, that's classified.*

When you start to dig into the history and functioning of the nation's premiere "cryptographic" (as in "code-breaking") intelligence organization, you quickly come up with a thoroughly disturbing fact: Most Americans know almost *nothing* about the giant combine at Ft. Meade, Maryland where thousands of computer-armed techno-spies spend their days trying to intercept millions of phone calls and emails and radio-TV signals from all around the globe.

In spite of the secrecy which surrounds NSA's operational procedures, however, one thing does stand out clearly: the stern prohibition – mandated several decades ago by the U.S. Congress – against using NSA's super-powerful electronic tools to conduct espionage against American citizens going about their ordinary lives in this country.

Created in 1952 as the hush-hush brainchild of the U.S. Department of Defense, NSA has from its very first day been warned about the dangers of misusing its vast communications espionage network in order to snoop on the domestic citizenry. And indeed, the strictures against such an abuse of power were carefully enumerated in the Presidential Executive Order (No. 12333) which authorized the creation of the intelligence hub.

According to 12333, the agency is limited to collect information that involves "foreign intelligence or counterintelligence" – and is specifically barred from gathering any data that describe the activities of citizens within the U.S.

Unfortunately, however, that strict regulation has sometimes been ignored by short-sighted politicians and intelligence officials determined to gain the info they want at any cost. Who can forget the abuses that occurred under former President Richard M. Nixon, for example . . . during an era when White House officials (including former Secretary of State Henry Kissinger) routinely winked at the law and ordered illegal wiretaps on their political enemies?

The Nixon offenses were disgraceful, of course. (They were also a major part of the investigation that eventually drove him from office in 1974). But they paled in the face of a wide array of abuses that reportedly began to occur after the devastating terrorist attacks of September 9th, 2001.

Determined to prevent further attacks – and also to apprehend the 9/11 plotters and bring them to justice – the administration of George W. Bush allegedly authorized "warrantless" wiretaps against U.S. residents within the nation's borders in what appeared (according to the New York *Times* and other publications) to be a clear-cut violation of the regulations that outlawed such domestic spying. And although the White House lawyers argued strenuously that the President's Constitutional obligation to protect the country "overrode" the Fourth Amendment protections against the domestic wiretaps, the consensus soon became overwhelmingly clear: *domestic spying on U.S. citizens is illegal, unless the government first obtains the appropriate "probable cause" warrants from the Foreign Intelligence Surveillance Court.*

This was the tangled background, then, against which the burly football player and intelligence analyst from suburban Baltimore would find himself struggling in 2002/2003, after he came upon information which clearly suggested that NSA was breaking the law with millions of domestic wiretaps.

As the struggling and increasingly alarmed Tice would eventually tell ABC News, during a momentous interview that helped to seal his fate as a whistleblower: "We need to clean up the intelligence community. We've had abuses, and they need to be addressed."

A SUDDEN AWAKENING: SPRING, 2003

Ask Russell Tice to tell you how he began to realize that NSA was illegally tapping America's telephones – along with many other tools for transmitting communications and data – and this broad-shouldered, thoughtful patriot will choose his words carefully.

"I can't get into too many specifics," says the hard-charging whistle-blower, "because I'm not allowed to discuss classified material with any-one – and that includes my wife, to say nothing of newspaper reporters or buddies at the bar during happy hour. But this much I can tell you: I was working on some information related to our ongoing effort to identify in-telligence targets who might want to attack Americans – whether here in this country or somewhere abroad – when I began to come across some continuing intelligence intercepts that looked highly dubious."

Describing the moment, Tice remembers sitting in his gray-painted cubicle at the agency's enormous headquarters building in Ft. Meade and staring at a glowing computer screen. The classified files he was reviewing that day contained information related to ongoing surveil-lance of "high-risk targets" – American citizens who were considered to be potential terrorism threats. "As I worked on this crucially im-portant task," he remembers, "I learned of this illegal and unconstitu-tional behavior through verbal communication with the source of the collection.

"You didn't need a Ph.D. to understand that if one [tapped] tele-phone caller was located in Kansas City and the other one was talking on a cell phone in downtown Cleveland, and both were U.S. citizens, then the monitoring had to be off-limits . . . if there wasn't an accompa-nying electronic search warrant, that is.

"But there were no such warrants in the record, none at all. I re-member sitting at my desk and just staring at the bare wall of his base-ment office and asking myself over and over again: 'What is happening to my country?' I love this country," he says quietly, "and I feel a deep sense of responsibility about the oath I took when I first joined NSA. That oath charged me with protecting the Constitution of the United States of America. I'd been doing that for several years, already, while serving honorably in the U.S. Air Force, and I took the oath very seri-ously. I went through an internal struggle for some time.

"When I realized that we were repeatedly violating the rights of our own citizens in order to defend the country against potential ter-rorists, I became deeply conflicted. Nobody wants to prevent another

9/11 anymore than I do – but you can't accomplish that by violating the right to privacy.

"If you start giving up our fundamental Constitutional rights as a means toward the end of national defense, you'll eventually find that there's nothing left to defend. I thought that was the wrong way to go about stopping terrorism then, and I still think it's the wrong way to go. That's why I decided to blow the whistle – and that's a decision I will stand by, no matter what happens to me in the end."

Although many of Tice's critics insist that he decided to blow the whistle because of "personality conflicts" with his superiors (or because he's "mentally unstable"), the highly regarded New York *Times* reporter James Risen – who worked for more than a year on the Tice case – concluded that the Maryland truth-teller and his fellow-whistleblowers were some of the most dedicated and thoughtful sources he has ever interviewed. As Risen pointed out in a recent interview, while also noting that *all* of the whistleblowers he interviewed for his story were truthful and reliable:

"Well, you know, I think this was the most classic whistleblower case I've ever seen where people . . . in a lot of stories, people have mixed motives for why they talk to reporters. For some of the people . . . there's a turf battle going on, and they're losing out in the turf battle, or whatever. But in this case – I've been a reporter for about 25 years, and this was the purest case I ever saw of a group of whistleblowers coming forward."

For "Russ" Tice, who describes himself as "a perfectly ordinary guy with no inflated ideas about my own importance in all of this," the discovery that his employer was engaging in daily lawbreaking came as a deeply disillusioning blow. "I remember this awful feeling I got, when I saw what we were really doing," he says today. "I'd been raised to believe that America could do wrong – and that there was no higher calling than to serve your country – except maybe to serve God – whether it was in a military uniform or as a volunteer.

"And then one morning I woke up to the discovery that not everybody shared my sense of idealism about America . . . and that there were bureaucrats in the U.S. Government who were willing to cheat on the rules and regulations in order to boost their own careers and win a promotion."

Tice says he became "discouraged and angry" – and that he had headaches so bad he could not sleep. He seethed in anger for many months, until he finally realized that he was "going to blow a gasket" and kill himself if he kept up his extreme anger. In order to survive, he had to "do other things" and "not think about what NSA was doing to me." He also insists that the psychologists who interviewed him during "fitness for duty exams" which were insisted upon by NSA were "way off the mark" when they concluded that he was showing signs of "paranoid psychosis."

He also notes the fact that nine months before "discovering their very dirty and unconstitutional crimes against the American people," he had visited the "psych office" at NSA for his routine "psych evaluation" – and he had passed with flying colors . . . just as he had passed every *other* psych exam he ever took at NSA and in his intelligence career. He says that when NSA found out about his snooping into their illegal surveillance, the agency called him in for an "emergency psych evaluation so that they could classify me as 'crazy'. Their purpose was simple: They did it in order to neutralize me, in case I went to the press.

"But the idea that I'm crazy is just plain ludicrous," he says today. "I've been a functioning adult for the past 20 years, and I've gotten excellent job-performance ratings in every federal job I've ever held, along with many awards for excellent service. What the federal government was really trying to do was to discredit me – by making it look like I was crazy. And they did it right after they realized that I'd found out about the illegal wiretaps. They wanted to punish me and make me grovel to get my job back – while also promising to keep my mouth closed about what I knew, forever. They wanted to break me."

The record bears Tice out. As several commentators have noted in recent years, he received several promotions and pay-raises prior to his decision to go public with reports of NSA wrongdoing. He also has a closet full of commendations from the Defense Intelligence Agency (where he worked for nearly four years and was the liaison to NSA for "black" programs). While working at Bolling Air Force Base for the

DIA, he spent a great deal of time doing tasks with NSA . . . and was then returned to NSA duty full-time as a regular employee in 2002.

Tice received numerous good-conduct and high-performance citations from the United States Air Force, as well as being honored for outstanding performance at NSA for his role in the Iraq conflict . . . and several of these awards were proposed during the same period in which the retaliation against him began to occur. Tice had also received an award from NSA for his outstanding work during the first Gulf War, in 1991-92.

"As long as I kept my mouth shut and went along with the program, I could do no wrong," he says with a note of bitterness creeping into his voice. "But as soon as they discovered that I'd found out about the law-breaking, the retaliation began. It was because I decided not to fold under the pressure and go along with the NSA abuses that they started saying I had a screw loose. And that's hardly a new tactic – it's the same method they use on many who dare to tell the public about what really goes on behind the closed doors at Fort Meade."

Describing the reprisals he faced after telling the New York *Times* about the illegal surveillance on Americans that was taking place regularly at NSA, Tice told the House Subcommittee on National Security that he had been subjected to a long list of abuses. As his testimony shows, that list contains a harrowing catalogue of punishments that were the result of speaking out. Here's a brief summary from his testimony on Capitol Hill on February 14, 2006:

"[The actions by NSA] included . . . surveillance by the FBI; denials from NSA that monitoring [of his phone calls] was being conducted; being placed in Purgatory at the Agency motor pool, where I was told little about my status; denying access to my own security and personnel files; evidence of FBI and NSA security documentation being hidden from the Office of Personnel Management; official complaints about psychological abuse being disavowed and their records vanishing; an agency security officer sent to my home to threaten me in person with dire consequences if I talked to the press; being banished from all Agency facilities even the non-secured spaces; being denied Freedom of Information Act for my own unclassified files for reasons of criminality and privacy rights; having my good name slandered and mistruths invented about me as a means to justify revoking my security clearance; the agency blatantly violating their own regulations and directives in order to ensure an adequate defense could not be mounted; being sent to a remote Agency warehouse where I was forced to perform back-breaking labor in a last-ditch attempt to force me to resign, and finally, I was subjected to a classic kangaroo court clearance revocation hearing where the same individuals maligning me were members of the panel and their names withheld, concealing their identities."

In a loud and assertive voice, the fearless Tice went on to tell the committee that "when I first contacted a senatorial, congressional representative, the agency was furious that I had 'gone off the reservation' and I heard that I would 'pay dearly.' Soon after that, I learned that the security office at NSA had quashed an award for my outstanding intelligence support involving the military action in Iraq.

"When I wrote one hundred and thirty-two letters to congressional members involved in oversight about the abuses of the NSA's security office, six days later a memorandum was written by security to have my security clearance revoked. After I spoke on Capitol Hill to congressional staffers from both the House and Senate about the abuses of the National Security Agency, four days later I was told that I was to be removed from federal employment.

"This is the contempt by the NSA that was shown for congressional oversight of intelligence."

Tice then noted that he had not been given "substantive options for reporting the injustices" that had been inflicted on him as a whistleblower. As he informed the astonished committee that day: "I did not approach my agency's inspector general's office because I knew they were co-opted by the security office. Instead, I attempted to work within the agency's chain of command, including personally talking to the deputy director, to no avail.

"I spent a considerable investment of my time on filing a complaint with the Department of Defense Inspector General's newly established office of Civilian Reprisal Investigations. These hopes were dashed when the National Security Agency's inspector general was tasked to conduct the investigation regarding the revocation of my clearance. The results were a predictable whitewash that was to be expected from a subordinate element entrusted to investigate its own taskmasters."

What followed, according to the struggling Tice, was a nightmare straight out of Franz Kafka's classic novel of bureaucracy run amuck, *The Trial.* As he told the panel of House members: "I was fortunate that I was allowed to take my case to the Merit System Protection Board because of my military service, yet the judge did not allow me to argue the merits of the security clearance – not even as they pertained to due process. The judge also denied most of my discovery requests to include my own personnel files from all the agencies involved.

"The NSA's lawyers asserted early on that the intelligence agencies were exempt from the provisions of the Whistleblower Protection Act – and that, even if it were established that I made a protected disclosure under the Intelligence Community Whistleblower Protection Act, the Act had no provisions to punish an agency for retaliating against the disclosure."

For Russell Tice, the die was now cast. Out of work and with little hope of ever being reinstated (or of recovering his former security clearance), he would end up living on unemployment and then working a long series of part-time jobs in order to put food on the table and help meet his house payments.

Explaining how all of this could happen in the "land of the free and the home of the brave," Tice told the chagrined members of the House panel on reform in government: "The ultimate reason that abuses are taking place is due to the lack of accountability within the Intelligence agencies. Whistleblowers are kept in the dark on purpose, with few legitimate avenues open for them to counter full-court press efforts by their own agency to retaliate against them for whistle-blowing, even while these same agencies pursue lip-service policies that require reporting waste, fraud, abuse and illegalities.

"As the situation now stands, national security agencies are left to police themselves and there is no incentive to do so. Whistleblowers inherently are pointing out wrongdoing that likely will embarrass their agency. This and the fact that the Intelligence community

Whistleblower Protection Act apparently has no enforcement provisions are allowing wrongdoers the freedom to retaliate with impunity.

"Those that retaliate need to know they will be held accountable within the intelligence community. The Whistleblower laws on the books need to be amended to include stiff enforcement . . . and the investigation of retaliation for whistle-blowing must be removed from the intelligence agencies."

As the long day of testimony finally ended, many of the House members on the committee were deeply moved to hear Russell Tice make his case loud and clear.

"The current system of whistleblower protection in the national security agencies is worse than nonexistent," said the courageous truthteller, "because it gives those who would report wrongdoing a false sense of security, believing the laws that exist will protect them. The truth is that they will not!

"When all avenues for protected reporting of waste, fraud and abuse are closed, or will ensure retaliation, people are either forced to remain quiet or to resort to drastic measures such as going directly to the press."

Perhaps the strangest thing about Russ Tice's amazing journey as a whistleblower is the fact that he knows he acted out of *patriotism* – out of a sincere love for his country. Far from trying to knock America down, he was seeking to protect what he sees as our most valuable possession by speaking out against the illegal surveillance that was taking place at NSA.

But he paid a brutally high price for his willingness to speak out. "It hasn't been easy, not having a full-time job. And losing my security clearance – that was probably the toughest part of it all. It takes a great deal of self-reliance and self-discipline to keep from getting depressed. You also have to be very careful not to try and ease the pain and anger with alcohol or other substances – because that approach can easily lead to dependence or outright addiction.

"Right now I just feel very grateful for the fact that I have a very loyal and supportive family behind me. Whenever I get down or get into a rage over it, I realize all over again just how fortunate I am to have so many people helping me get through the day. And I also realize that it's very important for potential whistleblowers to understand that doing is this is an extremely challenging and difficult proposition.

"I would urge people *not* to blow the whistle until they've thought long and hard about the consequences and made sure that they're willing to undergo the penalties and reprisals that usually follow."

As a counselor who has tried to help hundreds of whistleblowers over the years, I wasn't surprised to discover – soon after Russ Tice called me and asked for advice a few years ago – that he was quite lucid and down to earth about his case. Far from being the "paranoid" personality that NSA had warned about, he struck me as a solid citizen with a clear understanding of the issues that were involved in his situation with an employer who had clearly fired him as a reprisal for his whistle-blowing. After counseling him at length, I must say that I was impressed with his thoughtful, balanced view of his situation and his emotional strength.

Even though Tice was obviously sane and functioning at a high level, NSA appears to have done its best to suggest that he was, in fact, a deranged malcontent. According to the whistleblower, after he learned that NSA was illegally and unconstitutionally spying on US citizens, he was contacted by NSA's security office and ordered to undergo an emergency psychological evaluation. This demand was made even though he'd successfully completed his most recent routine psychological evaluation only nine months before.

The examiner was John Michael Schmidt, according to Tice, who also notes that the evaluation appeared to have nothing to do with mental illness concerns – and everything to do with retaliation.

Schmidt reportedly gave Tice a month to consider his supposed illness . . . and Tice understood that this was the timeframe within which he was supposed to confirm that he would never bring the subject of illegal phone taps up again. In other words, he was never to discuss what he'd learned about NSA's crimes against the American people.

Tice refused to back down, however – and he says that Schmidt promptly wrote that he was suffering from "Paranoid Ideation". Tice knew this was a lie – and he wasn't surprised when the lie was used to strip him of his security badge . . . even though he showed no clinical signs at all of "paranoia" on the Minnesota Multiphasic or any other tests.

Tice is also quick to point out that after he complained to his congressional representative, NSA sent him to another security-controlled psychologist, Marianne Moran. She conducted further testing that also showed no signs of mental illness. After determining that Mr. Tice occasionally made out to-do lists of things he wanted to achieve each day at work, and that he was very strict

in following security procedures (while also remaining very dogged at finding the answers to analytical intelligence related questions), Ms. Moran told him that he had an "Obsessive Compulsive Disorder".

He says he informed her that she was incorrect about this. But Ms. Moran's written report also included the term "Paranoid Disorder," even though there had been no mention of it in the conversations she'd had with him.

Tice also believed she was pressured by the NSA security office to include something to support Schmidt's lie. And Tice also notes that two other NSA psychologists had found he had no mental illness at all. As a result, Tice felt certain that the findings of mental illness were simply contrived retaliation for not complying with NSA's illegal and unconstitutional actions.

After additional measures of retaliation, Tice communicated with other NSA employees who were dismayed that they had also been trapped into involvement in NSA's criminal domestic spying, and then he contacted the press to expose the agency for their crimes.

He still believes that NSA's original intent to falsely paint him as mentally ill was based on two strategies. The first was to use the finding as a means to have him fired, which is what occurred. The second was to ensure that if he went to the press, they would tell the news media that he was crazy and could not be relied on as a credible source. NSA later told reporters that NSA would never spy on millions of Americans' domestic communications – and that this accusation also showed Tice was crazy.

To this day, he believes that both Schmidt and Moran were used by NSA's security office to stamp the "crazy label" on his forehead. And he says it worked, at least for a while; during those years when Tice was the only public NSA whistleblower associated with the allegations of NSA domestic warrantless spying, many in the press seemed disinclined to believe his reports of NSA crimes – thanks to the malpractice lies of Schmidt and Moran that Tice says took place during his long struggle to warn the public about the illegal spying.

In a recent interview with *Reason* magazine, Tice did his best to describe the fierce loyalty he feels to the Constitution of the United States. He also sought to explain that although he blew the whistle on the George W. Bush administration for spying on Americans, he actually believes that Russ Tice is a patriot. He also believes that Bush should have been impeached – and that he "needs to go to jail" over this issue.

As he told *Reason*: "I voted for this guy. I've always given him the benefit of the doubt. I didn't like the Patriot Act; I don't like a lot of what I've seen. But I've always felt that this president, in his heart, felt he was doing his best to protect the American people. I thought the Patriot Act was unconstitutional, but I've always given him the benefit of the doubt. I'm certainly hoping that he's been misled, and that if a broad-brush approach was used that the president wasn't aware of it or didn't understand the ramifications of, that hundreds of thousands if not millions of Americans [actually had] their rights violated [without his approval].

"But if that happened and the president knew totally the extent of it, and everything we're hearing now is just damage control from the White House – well, some time ago, we impeached a president for cheating on his wife, which as far as I'm concerned should've been between his family, his wife, and if he believes in one, his God upstairs.

"When it comes to high crimes and misdemeanors, knowingly and willingly doing *this* and then being arrogant about it and saying we're going to continue doing it – I would certainly think falls into that category of high crimes. People think it's not going to affect them. They think it's against the bad people, it's to protect our national security. Maybe it's against the law, but it's just the bad people, just to keep the terrorist from blowing up my neighborhood dam.

"But if those people find out it was hundreds of thousands or millions, and they were swept up into it and the government was listening to their conversation with their doctor – now all of a sudden it affects them personally. Right now I don't think people see how it affects them. Though even if it were just these few thousand people that have been talked about, nonetheless it's wrong. There's no reason that two thousand warrants could not have been done through the FISA court. The question is: Why wasn't it done?"

In a recent interview for this book, Tice also waxed eloquent about his motivation in blowing the whistle on the illegitimate surveillance. "In a very real sense, I honestly believe I was simply trying to follow the Boy Scout Oath we learned. We were taught that when you raise your hand and take an oath, that's your word. And your word is who you are.

"If you break your word, if you lie, as a person you're not worth much. In the intelligence service, you raise your hand and you take an oath to the Constitution of the United States. Not to the President, and not to the Classifications Officer, and not to the directors of federal agencies – but to the Constitution. That's what you are tied to, and that's what you are responsible to uphold. And that, ultimately when it came to down to a decision for me, that was the decision.

"It was all about keeping my word."

Epilogue

For years I have warned people not to blow the whistle without legal representation and to follow this plan.

A Guide to Effective Whistleblowing

Ten Important Things to Consider *Before* You Decide to Blow the Whistle

1. Are you ready to put your career on the line? Talk to your family and friends so that they can be with you when the times get tough.

2. Decide which of the alternatives you can use to solve the problem. For example, will your superior retaliate against you? If so, then don't tell that person. Is there a confidential way to pass along the information to the proper authorities so that an investigative group can take some action? The ethical functioning of the government or corporation is the responsibility of all persons in the organization. If you are the only one with the information you will become the target of an investigation.

3. Keep a log or diary of all facts or insights about the case. If legal testimony is inquired at some point, this log may be helpful in constructing a chronology of events. Identify your supporting documents before

you draw attention to yourself. Afterwards may be too late! Once you blow the whistle, records may disappear and not be accessible to you.

4. Identify your support groups – such as elected officials, non-profit organizations, journalists, church or social clubs, professional organizations and others. If you do not have a group behind you, whistle blowing will be a lonely uphill battle. Often these groups can act as third parties to speak to the press and others.

5. Before you go public with the information, attempt to carefully and informally talk with selected and trusted peers. Ask what they think about the problem. Remember that you will need to be tough-minded to "stick it out." Your witnesses and friends may be pressured to come forward with information against you, so the support of peers in addition to family and friends is extremely important.

6. Check with groups who work with whistle blowers for advice and support and to develop an action strategy for your case. The Whistleblower Support Fund (www.whistleblowing.us), the Government Accountability Project (www.whistleblower.org), the National Whistleblower Center (www.whistleblowers.org), and The Project on Government Oversight (www.pogo.org) might be helpful. Whistle blower cases tend to have similar legal strategies and building on the experience of others is helpful. Remember, though, that these groups usually have a waiting list of clients.

7. If you cannot think of a way to anonymously leak your information, talk with your attorney to determine whether your legal position is sound. You may also want to know the fees and up-front costs in case you need to file a lawsuit. This is extremely important! You may not have enough savings to cover legal costs.

8. Be on your best behavior. Once you blow the whistle, your supervisor and colleagues will be observing your behavior, so do not make your situation worse by breaking some obvious rule . . . for example,

by arriving late to work or to leave early. Be aware that support staff may be asked to observe you or security police may be used to investigate you.

9. Focus your disclosure on the facts rather than on an individual in the organization. Avoid pointing the finger at anyone. Rather let the disclosure itself leave a trail to the guilty party or parties.

10. Leak the information. Despite the controversy about leaks in Congress, all levels of government leak information. Since it is important to protect your identity, I recommend giving the information to a third party who will then leak the information. The task is to get the necessary information to the proper investigative group so that they can do their work. Attempt to keep out of the path of the inquiry. Don't be afraid to retreat.

D espite all my efforts to discourage blowing the whistle, most people come to me for help *after* they have "blown the whistle".

One's ability to protect their career from sure ruin is overshadowed by a whistleblower's overarching ethical value system to speak the truth to power. The stories are legion as we watch these brave whistleblowers follow their conscience and forget about their best career interest. But maybe their acts of conscience are the only answer to their dilemma of how to live with themselves in the face of great harm to one's fellow humans.

Maybe there is only a small chance that they will succeed. Nonetheless, it is often fixed in their minds that following truth and honesty is a greater value than the need to ignore or cover up waste, fraud and abuse of power.

As Jack Anderson stated in his March 24, 1985 column: "In a government that invests secrecy with a halo of national survival and treats dissent as disloyalty, a lonely hero occasionally rises up to thwart the wrongdoers. He belongs to that tenacious breed called whistleblowers, who are willing to risk personal harassment for the public good.

Here's Anderson's profoundly helpful column in toto.

From the Washington *Post*, Sunday, March 2, 1985

Jack Anderson

"WHISTLEBLOWER STRESS"

In a government that invests secrecy with the halo of national survival and treats dissent as disloyalty, a lonely hero occasionally rises up to thwart the wrongdoers. He belongs to that tenacious breed called whistleblowers, who are willing to risk personal harassment for the public good.

I have been dealing with whistleblowers for 38 years. They are often full of doubt and fear. They usually don't know just whom to go to or whether their disclosure will be taken seriously. Maybe, they fear, people will just yawn or even laugh at them for raising such trivial charges, and they will have exposed themselves for nothing.

"Whistleblower stress" can be traumatic, according to Donald Soeken, a 42-year-old government psychologist who counsels whistleblowers on his own time.

Soeken has treated hundreds of whistleblowers, including:

—-A Transportation Department worker who was falsely accused of mental unfitness and was summarily fired after she had exposed fraudulent padding of overtime claims;

—-An editor of a Health and Human Services Department publication who reported wrongdoing to a congressional committee and, thereafter, was fired on trumped-up charges that he was a brain-damaged alcoholic.

—-A woman who was labeled "unfit" by her superiors after she revealed their rampant sexual harassment.

Depression and anxiety are the two most common symptoms of "whistleblowing stress." Soeken starts the treatment by examining their documents sympathetically and helping them clarify their complaints. "The fascinating thing," he said, "once they're clear in their own minds, most of them say they'd do it over again but maybe a little differently. Basically, they're highly moral people with the conviction to stand up publicly for their beliefs."

Soeken confronts them squarely. "Why give in to the monster that wants you to succumb, to say you were wrong?" he demands.

He became interested in his rare specialty about 10 years ago when he noticed that a growing number of federal workers were being ordered to report to the Public Health Service for compulsory "fitness for duty" psychiatric examinations. "These people weren't crazy," he said, though some had become obsessed. "I discovered their conditions were symptoms of personality clashes or retaliation being taken against them."

I exposed this Soviet-style retaliation, and Soeken backed up my stories with testimony before Congress. This has stopped the compulsory, punitive psychiatric tests.

Some whistleblowers actually appear to be mental cases because of the symptoms associated with the stress they're enduring. "If you put anybody under enough strain, they'll show their weaknesses," said Soeken. "But that doesn't make them bad. The problem is that people don't look at the issue but at the symptoms, and say: 'How can you listen to this guy with problems?'"

For those with a dark secret to tell, who haven't yet blown the whistle but are already feeling deep anguish, Soeken has this advice: "I tell them not to do it publicly. I tell them to leak it. But I don't guarantee anything in terms of publicity or the effect on their family members."

C1985, United Features Syndicate

www.ingramcontent.com/pod-product-compliance
Lightning Source LLC
Chambersburg PA
CBHW051501170526
45166CB00001B/335